DR. DAVE McINTYRE

I GET IT NOW!

A GUIDE TO TEACHING AND UNDERSTANDING NOVELS USING CENTERLINE AS AN EXAMPLE

» NARRATIVE LLC «

Published by Narrative LLC
P.O. Box 11968
College Station, TX 77845

Copyright ©2014 Narrative LLC

Design and composition by Greenleaf Book Group
Cover design by Greenleaf Book Group

Cataloging-in-Publication data

ISBN 13: 978-0-9857929-4-7
E-Book ISBN: 978-0-9857929-5-4

First Edition

This book is dedicated to the best teacher I ever had:

Who taught me an eye for reading;

An ear for writing;

A love of learning;

A passion for logic;

A dedication to standards.

Who devoted every minute of her life to her students.

And never gave up on them, no matter what.

Thanks Mom.

CONTENTS

INTRODUCTION

FROM "I DON'T GET IT" TO "I GET IT NOW!"

"I don't get it."

Based on my experience in teaching for twenty-five years at the high school, undergraduate, graduate, and doctorial levels—with both civilian and military students—I believe that these are the four most devastating words a teacher can hear. They mean three things:

1 Despite the teacher's best efforts at conveying information he or she thinks is both interesting and important, the student does not understand the point the teacher is trying to make.

2 The student feels a passive-aggressive indifference to the material, suggesting not only that he or she does not understand it, but that they don't think it is *worth* understanding.

3   Especially when the teaching activity involves
    reading, unless teachers move quickly to help their
    students grasp both the *message* of the material
    and the *value* of that message, the whole exer-
    cise becomes counterproductive. An assignment
    intended to create a positive experience on the
    student's path to life-long learning, becomes
    instead another brick in the wall that separates that
    student from the collective wisdom of the past and
    personal success in the future.

This book is designed to use the novel *CENTERLINE*
as an aid to prevent that crisis from occurring with students, and to address it successfully if it does. To be clear—
this guide is *not* just about understanding *CENTERLINE*.
Instead the guide is designed to help readers understand
all literature—using *CENTERLINE* as an example. It will
help students prepare for other assignments that involve
reading, understanding, and writing about ideas in books,
essays, and on tests. It will help average readers discover
and enjoy a depth and richness they have been missing.

Why use *CENTERLINE* as the target text? Why not
just write the guide to focus in general on all literature?
Because *CENTERLINE* is a unique book. I wrote it as a
novel to be enjoyed, but also designed it as an example to
be taught. I incorporated advice from experts on the subject matter, but also applied my own experience as a teacher
of close reading and careful writing.

Unfortunately, the value of literature is not immediately
evident to many students. Some genuinely have trouble
navigating the words, sentences, paragraphs, pages, and

chapters that carry the author's message across time, space, and sometimes culture. For other students, "I don't get it" ("and I don't care to get it") is a learned response, adopted from hostile peers, apathetic parents, or even weak teachers. Either way, it presents a teachable moment—a turning point when the right teacher with the right book and the right tools can change the trajectory of a person's life.

"Oh! I get it now!" is every teacher's goal. It is the sound of a mind being opened and a life being changed. *CENTERLINE* is an intellectually exciting and emotionally engaging novel. This guide can help teachers make sure their students "get it," and having succeeded with this work, are ready to move on to similar success with other works.

The guide begins with a short discussion of literary criticism and analysis, followed by a brief explanation of foundational terms used to discuss the form and structure of novels. Then it offers some "tools of the trade" required to understand and discuss how authors convey their ideas to readers. Next it explains three questions that can be used to explore any novel. It applies those questions in a chapter-by-chapter analysis of *CENTERLINE*, using the previously taught literary tools, terms and techniques in the explanation. Each chapter analysis also includes my author's notes about how and why I crafted that chapter. The guide concludes with some ideas for teaching the novel in the classroom, and some alternative ways to think about literary analysis.

Please note that the guide is to be read in one order, and used with students in a different order. That is, users of this guide are offered frameworks and tools for analysis up front under the assumption that they are interested in learning the broad tools first and the specific application second. But I recommend that teachers reverse the process for students new to literary analysis. Allow them to read the book straight through, focusing on comprehension first. Let them enjoy the story and become hooked on the characters. *Then* teach the tools and frameworks that help them understand why they liked the book (or didn't), and use those tools to revisit the text to see how it works.

From years in the classroom, I know that the most gratifying experience a teacher can have is converting a resentful "I don't get it" into an excited "Oh! I get it now!" As the author of both the book *CENTERLINE* and this teaching guide, I am hopeful that teachers everywhere achieve that goal, benefiting their students in the process.

Dave McIntyre
College Station, Texas

WHAT IS *CENTERLINE*?

Wounded soldiers make a long trip from the pain and disorientation of a battlefield to the pain and disorientation of a homecoming.

Set at the height of "The Surge" in Iraq in 2007, the novel *CENTERLINE* tells the arresting story of the last leg of that journey through the eyes of patients, crew, and medical caregivers trying to make it home for Christmas. It is not an easy trip.

"Everybody who goes to war gets shot," one soldier says. "Some in the body. Some in the head. Some in the heart."

Air Evac 1492 is the Air Force call sign for the flight. Each person on board has an individual story of hopes, dreams, fears, and regrets as the aircraft wings its human cargo through bad weather, flashbacks, and in-flight emergencies. All are rushing toward an uncertain future.

CENTERLINE won the following book awards during 2013-14:

» Gold Award (First Place) for military fiction from the 2013 Next Generation Indie Book Awards, http://www.indiebookawards.com/.
» Finalist in the category of First Novel from the 2013 Next Generation Indie Book Awards.
» Gold Award (First Place) for military fiction for 2013 from the Stars and Flags Book Awards, http://www.starsandflags.com/.
» Bronze Award (Third Place) for 2014 Literary Fiction from the 2014 eLit Book Awards, http://www.elitawards.com/2014_results.php.

» Honorable Mention in the Genre Fiction category of the 21ˢᵗ Annual *Writer's Digest* Book Awards, http://www.writersdigest.com/online-exclusives/april-14/21st-annual-writers-digest-self-published-book-awards-winners.

CENTERLINE is available through Amazon.com, or through the website *http://www.centerlinethebook.com.*

NOTE: *All references to the novel in this guide apply to the printed version of the 2d edition, released by GoodBlood in 2013.*

WHO IS DAVE MCINTYRE?
(AND WHY SHOULD YOU LISTEN TO HIM?)

Dave McIntyre, author of *CENTERLINE* and this guide
to reading, teaching, and understanding novels, has taught
for more than a quarter of a century at the high school,
undergraduate, graduate, and DBA/PhD levels.

He graduated from West Point and spent thirty years
in the U.S. Army, retiring as a Colonel. His military time
was divided between duty with airborne and armored
reconnaissance units, and writing and teaching strategy
at the national level. He also taught English composition,
as well as English and American literature, at West Point.
He retired as the Dean of Faculty and Academics at the
National War College.

For two years after 9/11 he was deputy director of a
national think tank on homeland security, and for four years
directed a graduate program in homeland security at Texas
A&M University. He also taught national and homeland
security at George Washington University, the University
of Texas, and the National Graduate School.

Dr. McIntyre is presently a Distinguished Visiting
Fellow at the Homeland Security Studies and Analysis
Institute, in Falls Church, Virginia, and a lecturer at the
Bush School of Government and Public Service, at Texas
A&M University.

He has a BS in Engineering from the U.S. Military
Academy, an MA in English and American Literature
from Auburn University, and a PhD in Government and
Politics from the University of Maryland.

Other recent publications include:

- » A white paper on Risk Management for the Department of Homeland Security,
- » A national report card on security against Bio-Terrorism for the Bipartisan WMD Center (staff writer), and
- » *Business Continuity and Homeland Security, Vol. 1,* co-edited with William Hancock (Edward Elgar publishers, 2011).

HOW TO USE THIS GUIDE

I wrote *CENTERLINE* in the hope that people would be captured by the story, enamored of the characters, and moved by the message. But as an educator, I also wrote with two other goals in mind:

» To help teachers demonstrate literary analysis to their students;

» To help students appreciate the value of such analysis to their educational advancement, personal growth and future professional lives.

This guide directly addresses the second set of goals. Teachers and students who use it will find *CENTERLINE* not only a compelling story, but easily accessible to the tools of literary analysis. Successfully using those tools to form a deeper understanding of the book, the subject matter, and the human condition will boost student self-confidence for further reading and understanding of the literary world.

The secret to boosting students' understanding is twofold:

» Ensure they have a full understanding of the tools available for analysis;

» Provide a structured application of those tools to the book in a rewarding way.

To this end, I recommend that assignments be made in a different order from those usually found in literary study. All too frequently, students are commanded to learn literary form, structure, and analysis as they read. This causes them to lose track of the story as they immerse themselves in the details of new terms, and it prevents them from applying the tools taught last except at the very end of the story. It sucks the joy out of reading and replaces it with the drudgery of memorizing terms that can only be partially applied before the novel is finished and the class moves on. No wonder so many students are frustrated with the learning process.

If possible, I recommend reversing the standard teaching process—have students read the entire book before they analyze it. Assign as many pages of reading as practical before each class. Then in class discuss in detail what they read, using Question 1 (What happened?) from the Three Questions for Greater Understanding (Section 6) as a guide. Only after they have read the book, understand the narrative, and grasp the themes, should students be required to conduct a detailed literary analysis using the concepts presented as separate sections of this guide, to include:

» Section 2: The concepts of literary criticism and analysis,
» Section 3: The literary form of the historical novel,
» Section 4: The foundational structure of *CENTERLINE*,
» Section 5: Descriptive literary terms, tools, and techniques used for analyzing this specific novel.

If the students read the entire book first, concentrating on comprehension, then they can undertake a detailed literary analysis in which all Three Questions for Greater Understanding are addressed:

1 **What happened?** Do readers understand the events, thoughts, actions, etc. in the text?
2 **How did it happen?** How did the author manipulate the text to achieve the desired effects?
3 **What difference does it make?** How do the parts of the work tie together, and why should readers care about the text, techniques, and message of the book?

Instead of the frustration of trying to understand both the book and literary analysis one disaggregated piece at a time, students will receive a double positive reinforcement: enjoying the book as a whole, and *then* gaining a fuller understanding from holistic analysis.

For example, instead of learning about foreshadowing while in the process of reading the book, let the students see for themselves how information introduced early on creates suspense during the read, and an "ah-ha!" moment when they read the reveal. *Then* explain how the author used foreshadowing to achieve that effect.

As a specific example, after completing the entire book, students should be able to use the term *foreshadowing* to connect the discussion of a bleed air leak on page 4 of the Prologue; mention of a failed gauge on page 30 of Chapter 1; the failure and repair of a gauge in Chapters 3 and 4; and the indication of a continuing problem on page 179 of Chapter 7; all leading to a potentially catastrophic technical problem during the storm in Chapter 10. Viewing the book in retrospect, students will see how foreshadowing is used four times to build suspense and set up the drama of Chapter 10.

Here is another example using the idea of a *metaphor*. The mechanical problem with the aircraft reflects a larger theme in the book. Underneath many of the smoothly humming lives of people on the aircraft lurks some damage from the past—some wound that seems repaired or under control, but threatens at any moment to flash into a crisis that might prevent their ever returning to the centerline of their life. Like the aging aircraft, every wounded warrior aboard is a disaster waiting to happen. Only personal heroism and the actions of a dedicated team will get them home safely.

With skills and confidence thus acquired from such holistic analysis of this work, students will be able to address other works more quickly and with greater success.

CRITICISM VERSUS ANALYSIS

WHAT TO EXPECT FROM THIS GUIDE

Literary Criticism is a complex and sometimes convoluted field of study. It is as old as the first audience member who complained about some aspect of a tale told around a campfire. In its modern manifestations it is generally grounded in some "school" or set of theories about what a book or author should do, and how well a particular book or author meets that standard. It is fair to question whether any author can act as a proper critic of his own work. By the time a book is published, the author is simply too close to the story and the telling of the tale to properly evaluate how well his plan worked. Because I wrote both *CENTER-LINE* and this guide to understanding *CENTERLINE*, I will not attempt literary criticism of the book.

Literary analysis, on the other hand, refers to the detailed examination of the parts of a literary work, how they interact, and how they operate together to advance the work as a whole. An author schooled in literary analysis is uniquely positioned to use accepted analytical tools, terms, and techniques to explain how he or she intended the book to work, and what readers should look for as they read. So this guide takes a simple, straightforward approach to *traditional literary analysis*, which I define as *a rational, structured study of the various parts of a literary work, and the ways in which the parts are fitted together by the author and the readers, to create a meaning and a value greater than the sum of the individual parts.*

Traditional literary analysis is *not* a generally accepted literary term. But it *is* the approach most commonly used by general readers, mainstream teachers, and friends who might recommend books to one another. It assumes the following as essential elements of a valid study:

» **A designing author** (not just a disinterested observer) who uses form, conceit, setting, plot, characters, narration and other techniques to advance the story;

» **A crafted work** (not just collected musings), which may be examined using special literary terms and techniques;

» **Higher order meanings** (not disconnected observations), which include memorable concepts about the nature of life and mankind; and

» **Self-aware readers** who can evaluate their own response in terms of reason and emotion.

Also, traditional literary analysis accepts the idea that the effectiveness of a literary work may be enhanced by using humor or emotional rewards. Entertainment may even be the primary motivation of the author and main effect on the readers. To quote a character from *CENTERLINE*, "Does everything . . . have to have a crescendo? Some phony cosmic point?" (page 184).

Finally, traditional analysis assumes that there is value in understanding the "meaning" of the work as the author intended it. Evaluating the work depends primarily on the worth of that meaning, and how well the author conveyed it. However, traditional analysis also understands that no matter how universal the author may intend his or her message, cultural and historical context do influence the creation of the work, the delivery of its theme (message), and the perception of that theme by the reading audience— which may change over time. Consider, for example, Mark Twain's *The Adventures of Huckleberry Finn*. Initially dismissed by some as a thinly disguised plea for racial equality, it is now denounced by others as racially insensitive. Comments to this effect, informed by examples from the text, are a legitimate aspect of traditional literary analysis. So Critical Thinking, which recognizes the value of outside perspectives that may disagree with the author, and even with each other, is part of this traditional approach.

Of course, there are dozens of other schools of thought available to conduct literary criticism and analysis, ranging from Aristotelian to Marxist. Most are an outgrowth of the political and literary *zeitgeist* of their time. Students may gain valuable insights from reading *CENTERLINE* with these other approaches in mind. However, this guide is not designed to teach from those perspectives.

3

LITERARY FORM
(OR GENRE)

CENTERLINE AS A TYPE OF NOVEL

Literary works are generally grouped according to shared characteristics. The literary term for such groups is "genre." Sometimes those groups are defined by subject matter, as with comedy, and tragedy. Sometimes the dividing line is more a matter of structure. Prose, for example, is recognized by sentences, paragraphs, etc., written according to standard rules of grammar. At one time, poetry was also defined by aspects of structure such as rhyme or meter. But today works with clever or imaginative language might be included in poetry, even if written in free verse. So while the concept of grouping works into genres is helpful to students and analysts, authors are constantly challenging the boundaries between groups, making identification by genre an increasingly tricky proposition.

Within the confines of a genre, literary works may be further grouped by additional shared conventions or characteristics, or even subject matter. Works that fit the genre of "novel" but are about the American Old West (Zane Grey) are usually quite distinct from novels written about detectives (Mickey Spillane), or lawyers (John Grisham), or the people of sweeping geographical locations (James Michener). There is no end to this continuing subdivision of characteristics, and no name for the process either. The genre of novels has spawned the genre of detective novels, which has spawned the genre of female detective novels, which has spawned the genre of gothic female detective novels . . . and the process continues.

Still, students and readers need some sort of a hand-hold on the nature of a work in order to establish expectations. They can then analyze whether the book meets those expectations and how. I find the term "form" useful in describing the approach an author takes to presenting his subject matter within a given genre. Usually an author writes with a specific form in mind so that readers know what to expect when they buy the book. There are many forms of novels, and the list continues to grow as authors become more imaginative in combining earlier forms. Here are some examples of well-recognized forms for novels:

> » **Autobiographical:** Where the author supposedly tells his own story (e.g., *Great Expectations* by Charles Dickens).
> » **Journey:** Tracks the intellectual or emotional progress of the main character(s), frequently in

conjunction with a trip or passage of time—like a trek across country or progress through a school year (e.g., *Grapes of Wrath* by John Steinbeck).

» **Manners:** Where the dramatic tension is provided primarily by social rules and behavior which drive and constrain the characters. (e.g., *Pride and Prejudice* by Jane Austin. Her works are also sometimes considered romances as well. See below.)

» **Episodic:** When the narrative progresses through a series of independent encounters or "episodes," each of which advances the action and develops the main character (e.g., *Don Quixote* by Miguel de Cervantes).

» **Realistic:** Emphasizes the harsh, unfair conditions of real life, sometimes intended to generate a consensus for social change among readers (e.g., *The Jungle* by Upton Sinclair).

» **Romance:** Traditionally a story built on a fanciful tale and better than real-life characters, perhaps including lofty ideals, exotic settings, fantastic events, heroic behavior, etc. In more modern usage, a romance novel suggests deep and extended emotional interplay (romantic love) between male and female characters. (*Ivanhoe* by Sir Walter Scott is an example of a traditional romance. A novel by Danielle Steel is a modern romance. The lines dividing categories are not always clear.)

» **Fantasy:** A novel set in an imaginary world usually marked by magic, fantastic creatures, and characters with special powers. Fantasy novels frequently (but not always) include a romantic (in the traditional sense) theme (e.g., the *Harry Potter* series by J.K. Rowling).

» **Science Fiction:** Sometimes paired with Fantasy because both play out in a fantastic, imaginary setting (like another world or in the future.) However, Science Fiction is generally based on scientific concepts, although taken to extraordinary lengths in time and space. (*2001: A Space Odyssey* by Arthur C. Clarke is a classic example.)

Many other forms, such as Westerns and Detective novels (already mentioned), exist.

CENTERLINE is identified by genre as a novel, because it is an extended work of prose built around a core narrative. That is, all elements of the story line are related, and none of the sub-parts of the story can stand alone. This is different, for example, from collections of short stories that might all share characters, locations, themes, etc., in common, but each of which can be read and understood in full by itself. (For examples of the latter, see Ray Bradbury's *The Illustrated Man,* or Ernest Hemmingway's *The Nick Adams Stories.*) The dominant narrative line in *CENTERLINE* is the trip home—the pilgrimage—by members of the military, all of whom (to include the air crew and medical team) have been wounded in some way by war. So at first glance, *CENTERLINE* would qualify by form (sub-genre) as a war novel.

But the novel is more than a simple story about combat. For example, the Epilogue echoes several aspects of the Prologue, such as the aircraft raising its wing to turn as though it were raising its wing to wave, and the clipped instructions of the pilot to the crew. Given the repeated examples of the pilot's cool professionalism and technical expertise throughout the book, the short scene in the Prologue might be expected to be part of a pattern. And so it is. Yet in the Epilogue, a different pilot is at the controls. The actions are the same, the dangers are the same, and the risks of future injury—physical, mental, or emotional—are the same. But in the Epilogue, the characters are different. The suggestion is that a cycle is continuing—a cycle of war, and wounding and homecoming. Yes, *CENTERLINE* is a war novel. But its form is more complex than that simple description would suggest.

In fact, *CENTERLINE* has a blended or **hybrid form**. It is a high-tech, action-adventure novel, set in a particular historical frame (a specific war), with emotionally engaging characters.

CENTERLINE is an **action-adventure novel,** but of an unusual type. In most action-adventure novels, what the characters *do* drives the story forward, rather than what the characters think or feel. Also, the line of action is usually straight ahead. The conflict is frequently of a single type: against an enemy, against the weather, against nature, etc. In more complex works, there may be an external conflict and an internal conflict between characters.

» In *CENTERLINE* there are multiple characters, multiple external conflicts (with the aircraft, with the weather, with physical wounds), multiple internal conflicts (within and between characters), and multiple lines of action (forward on the aircraft and backward through flashbacks). What the actors did, thought, and felt in the past, influences what they do, think, and feel in the present. All of this is played out in the present, in the face of a balky aircraft, a challenging mission, and a killer storm.

CENTERLINE is a **high-tech novel.** It offers the detailed, functional, almost engineering-like description of processes (like sailing a ship or attacking a submarine) required to move the action forward. (For example, Tom Clancy is well known for high-tech novels like *The Hunt for Red October.*)

> » In *CENTERLINE*, the high-tech activity is flying—specifically flying a large Air Force transport aircraft on routine missions, on combat missions, and in special circumstances (as in a storm or when under attack by missiles or rockets). The work also provides a detailed (and exciting) picture of the technical aspects of emergency and routine medical care, as well as ground combat in Iraq.
> » Compelling tactical and technical procedures are used throughout the book to drive the pace of the action. The technical competence of some characters (the pilot, the copilot, the nurse, etc.) is used to develop their personalities and the dilemmas that test their character.

CENTERLINE is a **historical novel,** in that it is set at a specific place and time, and those parameters are important to the telling of the story.

» This book plays out during "The Surge" in Iraq in 2007 ("a surge of troops into Iraq means a surge of casualties out" page 31), and in the middle of a long "Global War on Terrorism." This timing is important to the overall tone of the book. The crew and families and aircraft are tired of war and deployment. This historical setting is ironic in that readers know the war will last at least another seven years, but the characters do not. Furthermore, setting the novel specifically at Christmas raises the poignancy and emotional power of the story.

» Many historical novels set the actions or characters in proximity to a major historical figure (a president or a general) or action (Gettysburg or the D-Day landings). *CENTERLINE* takes place in a real historical setting, but without the sense of purpose or significance that would be implied by a major figure or event. The wounded are loaded into "a great logistical machine," and carried home on a "medical conveyer belt" (page 45). This makes the characters aboard Air Evac 1492 seem more human and more vulnerable, trapped as they are in a real but impersonal process. (Students might recognize the same technique of impersonal isolation from the larger actions and meaning of the war in Stephen Crane's *The Red Badge of Courage*.)

CENTERLINE is an **emotionally compelling** (some would say **romantic**) **novel**. The story is *pushed along* by the aircraft and its mission, and the various life-threatening challenges that the crew faces. But readers are *pulled along* by sympathy with each character's struggle to regain balance in his or her life, after losing it to the physical, mental, or emotional wounds of war. Readers are also engaged by a set of individual mysteries involving those characters. They want to know how each unfolding story will play out. The author uses several literary tools to heighten this emotional quotient of the story.

» One tool is the premise of the central story itself. A flight full of wounded, still bearing the pain of war, struggling with feelings of loss and guilt, heading home to an uncertain reunion at Christmastime, presents an emotion-laden story, even before the action begins.

» This sense of pain and loss is heightened by dramatic irony repeatedly introduced between the emotional reality portrayed in graphic flashbacks, and the false normalcy projected by characters as they stoically go about their duties of flying, nursing, counseling, or soldering on to recovery.

» The complicating factor of frustrated romantic love is interjected through three character pairs (pilot-wife, nurse-Ranger, and mechanic-reporter). All three pairs come across as star-crossed lovers, attracted to each other, but separated by barriers constructed from events in their past, and almost insurmountable in the present.

Constructing a novel with a **hybrid form** like *CENTERLINE*, designed for many different audiences, with many moving parts, is a high-risk endeavor. It could easily be pulled apart by the differing demands of technical descriptions versus action sequences, versus historical accuracy, versus poignant family moments and private emotional recollections. Additionally, a failure in any of these areas might crash the story as a whole.

What holds the narrative together is the sense of military mission—the fact that although characters or readers might wish to extend the emotion in one area or follow the action in another—the mission will brook no deviation from the flight plan. The trajectory is set. The story is moving. The characters are "en route." Readers can only hang on for the ride, experiencing each surprise along the way, and hoping for a safe return to the centerline.

4

LITERARY STRUCTURE

WRITING (AND READING) CENTERLINE

The author's conscious use of an intentional literary structure is one of the most important points to convey to students to help them "get" a novel. In fact, in order to achieve his or her desired effects, an author makes numerous decisions about the design of the story and its parts. What are these decisions? How do they work? Here is a partial list.

CONCEIT

This is the intellectual idea upon which the work is established. The conceit of *The Adventures of Huckleberry Finn* is that an unschooled boy from a slave state takes a raft trip down the Mississippi River with an escaped slave, thus learning about himself, the world, and his fellow man in the process. The conceit of *The Canterbury Tales* is that archetypical characters on a Medieval religious pilgrimage tell stories to pass the time; the characters (as readers meet them in the Prologue) provide richness to the stories they tell, and the stories give insight and depth to the characters who tell them.

The conceit of *CENTERLINE* is that the final leg of the trip home from war for wounded warriors finds them worrying about who they have become and how they will be received after their experiences in the combat zone. One major irony of this conceit is that the "wounded warriors" changed by war include not only the soldiers injured in the body, but also the air crew, medical teams, and families at home who have been wounded in mind and heart as well. A second major irony of the conceit is that those who learn most from the characters' trip back to the centerline of their lives are the readers themselves.

SETTING

Many people think of the setting as the place where the novel takes place, but it is more properly regarded as *the background against which action plays out*. It is important to understand, for example, that *CENTERLINE* is set at the height of "The Surge" in Iraq, when the public and the military (and even the equipment) are already weary from war. Yet deployments are rising, and burdens are increasing on both wounded and those caring for them back in the United States. The conflict between the pilot and his wife only makes sense against a background of continual family separation for years. The conflict (and ultimate resolution) between the nurse and the Ranger only makes sense against the background of loss that both have seen and felt. The chaplain's decision to leave the ministry only makes sense against the background of suffering he has tried to relieve during his tour in the combat zone. The tension of an uncertain homecoming for soldiers no longer whole gains additional power from the setting at Christmas, with its implied image of families whole and healthy.

The point for students to understand is that *every element of the setting is selected by the author and included on purpose* in order to advance the readers' experience with the novel.

Of course, sometimes readers bring their own perspectives to the story, giving the setting a different resonance from what the author intended. This can provide a good lead into a discussion of differing types of literary criticism.

PLOT

The concept of plot might seem simple. It is not.

This is because the order and description of events, their interaction with characters, and their outcome in the story are all elements subject to creative manipulation by the author. The plot is not just the way things happen in the story. It is the way the author crafted things to achieve his desired effect. In fact, *the plot is called the plot because the author must plot it out ahead of time.*

CENTERLINE tells a central narrative story about wounded soldiers, crew members, medical staff, and families all affected by aeromedical flights taking wounded home to recover. It involves more than two dozen characters and multiple plot lines. This point may be driven home by referring to the map, the table of contents, and the way the Prologue is matched with the Epilogue, Chapter 1 is matched to Chapter 11, Chapter 2 is matched to Chapter 10, and Chapter 3 is matched to Chapter 8. Chapter 9 breaks this pattern by design to provide both a surprise and a special emotional impact for the readers.

Here are some of the artistic choices available to an author in crafting a plot:

» **Sequence of Events:** The order in which events unfold. In *CENTERLINE*, events are expected to unfold with the predictability of a flight plan. This sequence is frequently interrupted by flashbacks, where past events push to the fore, because of their importance to the story and the individual character.

» **Flashback:** An interruption to the chronology of the narrative by a look back at previous events that explain a character's current actions. *CENTERLINE* uses this device extensively.

» **Climactic Scene:** A single moment toward which all precipitating action moves, and from which all falling action proceeds toward resolution. Because *CENTERLINE* has multiple plot lines, it has multiple climactic scenes.

» **Episodic Approach:** A framework built of individual events that affect the main actor and help to develop his or her character, but are largely unrelated by cause and effect. *Don Quixote* is an episodic novel—the old knight wanders the countryside and encounters many unrelated adventures. *CENTERLINE* is marked by many separate episodes, but they are all related to plot and character development by cause and effect.

» **Conflict:** A clash that stimulates the characters' actions in the story. The conflict may be physical, mental, emotional, with another character, with nature, or strictly internal. Selecting the conflict around which the story revolves is crucial. Without conflict, there is no novel. Because there are multiple characters and multiple story lines in *CENTERLINE*, there are multiple conflicts. Some are against nature and aging technology, as with the storm and the bleed air leak in the C-130. Some are between characters, as when the reporter seeks a story. Some are professional, as when medical crews strive to save burned Marines. Some are personal, as when the pilot and his wife strive to reconcile duty, guilt, and love.

» **Main Plot/Subplot:** A subplot is a subordinate story that runs through or alongside the main story, complicating the action and resolution. For example, in a crime novel, the lead detective might have a personal problem (an ex-wife, a short temper, an aversion to technology) that complicates the pursuit of the criminal. With its large number of characters and large number of conflicts, *CENTERLINE* has multiple subplots. All of them contribute to a single holistic theme: people whose lives have been thrown off center seek to regain "the centerline."

CHARACTERS

Novels are primarily about characters. Some literary works may emphasize the grandeur of the setting, the manners of the people, the power of nature, or some other aspect of the story. However, unless fictional characters are operating within the literary framework of an extended narrative, the work is not a novel. Thus the characters and their actions are supremely important to the success of the novel. Understanding what they do and why they do it is essential to understanding the core ideas of the novel itself.

The term *character* is frequently used to refer to the actors in the text, but *it more precisely indicates the **qualities** of the actor as a person.* This fact is most evident in works where one or more of the actors are designed to capture a particular quality or set of qualities, as when the actor is "the personification of" selfishness, generosity, or compassion. When the qualities are combined in such a way as to describe a recognized "type" of person, we call that an *archetype*—as in the Knight, or the Scholar, or the Pardoner from *The Canterbury Tales.*

At first glance, several of the actors in *CENTERLINE* might appear to be archetypes (the pilot, the nurse, the chaplain, etc.). However, the flashbacks and reveals give these major actors (and even some of the minor actors) an unexpected sense of depth and even pathos. *These people are not just bundles of representative qualities. They are the product of sometimes horrible experiences that have unbalanced them, and they struggle in ways the readers can identify with to overcome this influence and regain the* centerline *of their lives.* In fact, this internal struggle is the central action of the book, set against the external actions of the trip.

One of the most interesting questions for students to ponder in this novel is whether the individual actors succeed in this internal struggle. Who regains their centerline? Who does not? Why?

The rest of this guide will use the term *character* in its more modern sense, to describe the actors who play functional roles in the book. Still, the personal qualities of these characters deserve careful consideration and class discussion.

PLOT DEVELOPMENT

In 1863, Gustav Freytag, a German novelist, published a schematic explaining the structure of five act Greek tragic plays as a set of literary terms arrayed on a triangle. He further postulated that this structure could be applied to many novels and other stories. Still called Freytag's Pyramid (despite many modifications), Figure 1 helps students understand the predictable relationship between the various scenes and actions in traditional literary works of prose.

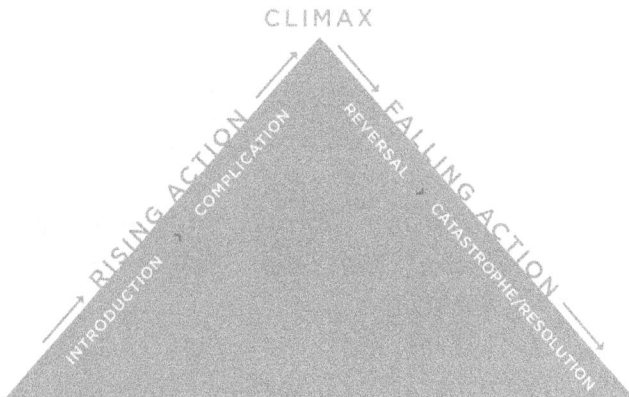

Figure 1. A Version of Freytag's Pyramid

» The *introduction* sets the scene, introduces the main characters, and establishes the conflict.

» The *complication* introduces the actions and factors that exacerbate the conflict.

» Taken together the rise in action and emotion from the *introduction* through the complication constitutes the *rising action.*

» This rise in action culminates in the *climax,* which is the moment of maximum emotion, when the dramatic tension is released.

» In a tragedy (defined classically as the fall of a person of high position), the actions following the climax describe a *reversal* of fortune.

» Actions following the reversal lead to the final collapse of fortune, call the *catastrophe* (or perhaps in a play that offers some sense of redemption, the *resolution*).

» The actions that connect the reversal to the catastrophe are called the *falling action.*

Many versions of this pyramid exist. One of the most common variations includes a flat line called *exposition* at the beginning (explaining the overall background for the tale), and another flat line called *dénouement* at the end (fully explaining the ending and the significance of the narrative).

A simple diagram may suffice to describe the plot development of formulaic Greek plays of 2,300 years ago, but capturing the holistic progress of complex modern plays and novels is more difficult. There are just too many characters, actions, plot lines, and complications to describe with a single line of action. Additionally, longer modern works may include new techniques, like the *reveal* (when some key piece of evidence explaining the action becomes apparent to the audience) or a *double* or even *triple ending* (when, for example, a villain previously thought vanquished appears on the scene again).

However, the concept of graphically portraying events and lines of action as the novel progresses is a good one for showing students how the subtle points of narrative choice by the author contribute to the progress and overall effect of the novel. In this guide, the concept of graphing the plot in *CENTERLINE* chapter by chapter in order to follow its development is mentioned frequently.

NARRATOR/NARRATION

The narrator is the person who tells the narrative—the speaker who recounts the story. *In some novels the narrator is one of the characters*; he or she tells the story in the first person, and comments upon it either with partial knowledge as it unfolds, or in retrospect with an understanding of what is coming next. *More common is the omniscient author* who is above the action and is able to explain what is happening as well as what the characters are thinking and feeling. A variation on this approach is *when the narrator lets the actions of the characters speak for themselves.* There are various other experimental approaches to narration. *The perspective from which narrative is related to the readers is called the point of view.*

CENTERLINE takes an unusual approach toward narration and point of view. Many of the characters are offered a chance to tell their stories (to the reporter character or through some other device) but refuse to do so, or tell a story that is only partially true. The author then steps in with a flashback to tell what actually happened. From this gap between outside truth and inside truth, readers perceive the discomfort, and in some cases anguish, of characters wounded in some way by their experiences in war, but unable to express what they feel. This sense of isolation, even from those the characters love, is itself another wound of war.

A clear example is the female mechanic who tells the reporter she will be met by a big family with lots of children, while she carries inside the knowledge that her wound will prevent her from having children of her own. What readers pick up from these varying versions of reality (presented from differing points of view) is the sense of fear and isolation the character feels at the prospect of disappointing a new husband who wants a big family, and of being the only one among the sisters in the family not to bear children.

With some CENTERLINE characters (the pilot, the copilot, the nurse, the one-armed writer), *the gap between perceived reality and "flashback reality" is progressive.* That is, it occurs more than once, revealing more about the characters' internal turmoil as the trip (and the story), continues. Many readers have commented that they felt "pulled along" by the story. ("I couldn't put it down" is a common comment.) Students should understand that this is not an accident, but a calculated decision by the author to create and resolve little mysteries as rewards for readers along the way. Why is the pilot driven to perfection? Why does the nurse lose herself in professionalism? Why is the copilot determined to succeed?

Often the culmination of this narrative disconnect between outside truth and inside truth is at *one cathartic moment of maximum emotion when some final piece of information is provided.* Screenwriters call this the *reveal.* An example comes in Chapter 10 when the copilot reveals how she still feels driven by and resentful toward a father, who had impossibly high standards.

Finally, this disconnect between the external character and the internal character revealed by flashbacks becomes such a pattern in this book that readers begin to expect it. Thus *when a reveal comes without the flashback set up* (as when the reporter reveals her background to the one-armed writer, page 200), it comes as a surprise (and another reward) to readers.

This whole discussion of narration and how various approaches drive the story and pull the readers provides an excellent opportunity for teachers to demonstrate to students that the craft of writing is more than simply putting words on a page. The author must have a plan, and must use tools of the trade to make the work memorable and worthwhile. With this awareness, students can reach into *CENTERLINE* and see how it works. Then they can use what they learn to read and write about other works in the future.

LITERARY TERMS, TOOLS, AND TECHNIQUES

CRAFTING CENTERLINE

Without a clear understanding of literary terms (sometimes called elements of style), readers do not know what to look for in a work, or how to describe what they think, see, and feel. Although many terms have been developed, every one in the abbreviated list below applies to *CENTERLINE* at some point in the text. More extensive lists are available in various academic texts.

Please note that some of the material from Section 4: Literary Structure is repeated here. This is intentional. Teachers, students, or general readers who want to use this guide to analyze works other than *CENTERLINE* can turn to this single section for consolidated help.

Allusion: A brief reference to a generally well known subject. An allusion may enrich a passage by establishing broader connections. In *CENTERLINE*, the direct and indirect allusions to Santa and *The Night before Christmas* (Chapter 4) reinforce the emotional impact of setting the story at Christmastime.

Analysis: The in depth study of a literary work by dividing it into parts (chapters, themes, characters, etc.), examining those parts in detail, then reassembling them to better understand how they work together to achieve the overall effect.

Archetype: A character that personifies the traits of a model or "type" person, based on the collective experience of many readers. The Knight in *The Canterbury Tales* is an archetype, as are the pilot, the nurse, the reporter, the Ranger, etc., *to some extent* in *CENTERLINE*. Note that Chaucer's archetypes were idealized to the point that they did not even have personal names; even the narrator was identified only as "the Host." In contrast, *CENTERLINE*'s "the pilot" acts as an idealized professional, but also has a home life, a history, and some problems he cannot solve. Dramatic effect is sometimes enhanced when otherwise archetypal characters act in unexpected ways. This is true of the pilot in Chapter 11.

Catharsis: This concept remains a matter of debate in literary circles. Traced at least as far back as the Greeks, the term describes the purging of strong emotions (especially of fear or pity) following a climactic (and especially a tragic) literary event. It should not be confused with a climax, which is the highpoint of action. Both the copilot and the readers experience a catharsis at the end of Chapter 9.

Characterization: A novel is fundamentally about the interaction of a human with other humans, places, or things.

Different types of novels may emphasize different aspects of this interaction. For example, a Picaresque is a (usually humorous) novel focused on the social interactions of a low character. Regardless of form, a novel's success depends on character development. This may be thin, focused on one main characteristic, or more rounded, drawing on various situations, decisions, and actions. It may be presented to the readers by direct description, character actions/interactions, or interior observations. The character's nature may remain fixed as the novel progresses, or it may change over time. Whatever else may be said about a novel, its success is determined largely by the readers' interest in the characters, which is determined by the author's skill at characterization.

Dramatic Structure: The framework around which a literary work is built (especially in a traditional play). The traditional pattern is: introduction, rising action, crisis (or climax), falling action, resolution. This structure is important in setting (and satisfying) reader expectations. Frequently, the pattern is changed for additional dramatic effect—especially if the work contains multiple major characters. In *CENTERLINE*, for the major characters in the rear of the aircraft, the climax, falling action, and resolution all take place in Chapter 8 when they arrive in Garden City. For the copilot, a crisis/climax occurs in Chapter 9 when she faces the realities of war. The crew as a whole faces a crisis/climax in the storm of Chapter 10. The family unit of the pilot and his wife face their crisis/climax in Chapter 11.

Flashback: A literary device whereby the author provides additional details by presenting an event that occurred before the beginning of the narrative. A flashback generally provides information essential to properly understanding a character's actions, motivations, or internal state. Flashbacks are used extensively in *CENTERLINE* to solve the mystery of a character's thoughts or actions. In Chapter 3, the female mechanic becomes quiet when the subject of children arises. A flashback explains that because of her wounds she cannot have children herself.

Foreshadowing: Details or actions provided by the author for the purpose of preparing the readers for future events. In Chapter 7 of *CENTERLINE*, after two replacements, the rpm gauge on the Number 1 engine flicks twice into the red zone during an otherwise routine climb out toward Garden City. The crew does not see this, but readers do, and wait in suspense for the problem that develops in Chapter 10.

Hero: Although the term has come to be identified in the popular mind with moral or heroic behavior, in a literary sense, it simply identifies the character with the greatest relationship to the action. The term *protagonist* suggests the same primary role for a character, but without the suggestion of admirable behavior (e.g., the protagonist in *The Godfather* is technically the "hero," but without admirable values). As with *The Canterbury Tales*, *CENTERLINE* contains so many major characters that it is difficult to identify a single hero. Some readers think of the pilot in this role. Others have suggested that the "hero" who really moves the action forward is The Hercules (The Herc)—the aircraft itself.

Imagery: Unfortunately, this word has various literary

meanings. In the broadest of terms, it is the tool the author uses to appeal to all the senses as though the readers were actually experiencing the action. Thus, images of sight, smell, hearing, etc., may be described in such a way that the readers are transported into the story in mind and emotion. *CENTERLINE* was written with a future screenplay in mind, so the imagery is intensely visual. Some readers report being moved to tears by the powerful images of the burned Marines in Chapter 9. Images may also serve a specific function in the narrative. Note how the image of the centerline is reflected on the cover, in the title, and repeated throughout the book. Clearly it is intended to perform a vital function—which readers and students may debate (see *metaphor, simile,* and *symbol*).

In medias res: Literally, "starting in the middle." The Prologue to *CENTERLINE* begins *in medias res* with the intense action of a high-speed, low-level, multiaircraft air drop mission, flown through the deep twisting valleys of Northern Arkansas. Readers are introduced to the characters, the aircraft, and the challenging life-and-death nature of military aviation, all in a way that pulls them into the cockpit and into the mission. This opening also establishes the tone and pace of an adventure novel so that readers will be prepared for the flying scenes that come later, after the situation and character development of Chapters 1 and 2.

Irony: A conscious technique used by an author to enhance the emotional power of a scene by drawing attention to the distance between what is said or thought, and what is actually taking place. There are numerous types of irony:

» **Dramatic Irony,** where there is distance between what the readers know or suspect, and what a character believes to be true. In *CENTERLINE*, Chapter 4, the pilot's wife tries to send a reassuring text, which the audience understands but the pilot takes as nagging and a lack of trust.

» **Situational Irony,** where one character understands a situation quite differently from another. In *CENTERLINE*, Chapter 6, the reporter thinks from the chaplain's answer that he did standard counseling in Iraq, but he was actually trying to comfort dying soldiers.

» **Verbal Irony,** where a character says or thinks one thing but the opposite is true. In *CENTERLINE*, Chapter 6, the nurse thinks her fiancé is committed to her, but he turns out to be already married.

Metaphor: An indirect comparison between two things without using *like* or *as*. This comparison increases the power of a passage by creating additional clarity, images, and emotions in the readers' minds. For example, in Chapter 10 of *CENTERLINE*, the pilot views the beauty of the stars from the high clear atmosphere on Christmas Eve, and is transported to "God's galactic cathedral"—a powerful metaphor for the peace and safety that he immediately wishes he could share with his wife. Then comes the moment of crisis, when he is pulled down "Into the Darkness" (chapter title) of a fierce winter storm—another metaphor for both the storm of his memories, and the storm of his home life.

Mood: The emotional attitude that the author establishes around the subject or theme of his work. Exploration of this term leads to the broader question, "What exactly is this book about?" *CENTERLINE* is set among a group of people damaged in body or spirit by war, and pushed and pulled irrevocably toward an uncertain homecoming at Christmas. Apparently, the intended mood is a combination of nervous excitement and somber uncertainty. Readers bring their own perspective to the work, so each might describe the mood in somewhat different terms (see *tone*).

Narration: A form of composition that directly relates an event (or related events) in a way that interests or entertains an audience. It may use the tools of an author's trade listed in this section, and many others besides. Other forms of composition include Argument (an effort to convince on one or more points), Description (an effort to recount the important aspects of a thing), or Exposition (an effort to explain the nature of a thing) (see *purpose*).

Narrative: The story that a narration tells. It generally has a point and a plot line that leads to that point. Some authors will intentionally confuse this structure for effect (e.g., Joseph Heller's *Catch 22*).

Novel: As a general statement, a long fictional narrative written in prose. Although some are completely detached from reality, most are set in a recognizable "real world." However, even then, a certain amount of "poetic license" is allowed with characters, settings, actions, etc. An example would be Ian Fleming's series of James Bond novels, grounded in the reality of intelligence operations, but free from the boundaries of historical (and sometimes even physical) reality. *CENTERLINE* is an exceptionally realistic novel where every character, location, and action could actually take place (and probably has).

Parallelism: The intentional structuring of literary elements (words, images, titles, etc.) to suggest equivalence or balance, or even completeness. One obvious example in *CENTERLINE* is the inclusion of both a Prologue and an Epilogue. Both jump into the action *in medias res.* Both chronicle the professionalism of a pilot amid the tension and pressure of a difficult mission. Both suggest life and death are on the line. Both emphasize action—the time for reflection (and perhaps regret) will be later. These elements suggest a further parallel: In the Epilogue, the inexperienced copilot of the novel becomes very like the experienced (and perhaps haunted) pilot of the Prologue. The parallel construction of these chapters suggests that a cycle continues.

Plot: The way in which the scenes of the work are arranged to convey the whole of the action. Some more traditional readers believe that this ordering (plotting) of events is the most critical element of a novel, because they see the novel as a series of cause-and-effect moments that drive toward a logical conclusion. Over time, opinion has changed on this matter, with some now arguing that Characterization is more important than plot, or even that the apparent randomness of events in a story (carefully thought out by the author, of course) conveys a truer version of life than does a "documentary" collection of true, but more scripted moments. In *CENTERLINE*, the plot results from a combination of these factors. The map shows the carefully planned missions as they were intended. The events of the chapters show how fate intervenes. Furthermore, what appears to be a well-defined plot line is constantly interrupted by flashbacks showing that the cause and effect in each character's life is not what readers expect at all. Thus what appears to be a very simple plot becomes quite complex because of the depth and variety of the characters involved.

Prologue: A very old (Greek and Roman) technique of allowing an outside "voice" to set the context for the audience (readers) by providing details about the setting, characters, etc., essential to understanding the work. Although Shakespeare used Prologues effectively, the most famous example in English literature is in *The Canterbury Tales*. There Chaucer described the season, the trip, the game, and the travelers who would interact during the rest of the work. With that basis, readers could understand the double message provided by the nature of each character and the tale that he/she told. The Prologue to *CENTERLINE* does something similar but in a different way. In order to understand the later parts of the novel, the audience needs to know something about the characters who comprise the crew, their duties, and the dangers and technical challenges of their missions. Just as Chaucer used his Prologue to set the overall story as part of a pilgrimage, *CENTERLINE* uses the Prologue to introduce the importance of getting back home to the safety of the centerline.

Protagonist: The main character of a literary work. The word is almost interchangeable with **hero,** but is used to emphasize the objective nature of the application to any particular character. Billy Budd was the hero of Herman Melville's novel by the same name, as a main character who demonstrated traits of moral heroism. Murderers Dick Hickock and Perry Smith were the protagonists of Truman Capote's "non-fiction novel" *In Cold Blood*. Jim has been called the protagonist (vice hero) of Joseph Conrad's *Lord Jim*, because of this main character's cowardly act early in the book. But some analysts call Jim a hero, arguing that his moral behavior redeems him in the end. Whether any single character should be identified as the hero or protagonist of *CENTERLINE* is open to discussion.

Purpose: The goal the author is trying to achieve by writing the book. This is not always accepted as a standard literary term, but it is very useful in discussing works with students or readers new to novels. Rarely does an author clearly state the purpose of a book in the work itself. Rather, the purpose must be deduced by literary analysis.

Realism: The accurate-to-life portrayal of the major elements of a work such as a novel. Realism arose as a reaction against excessive Romanticism (marked by the triumph of emotion over reason). Over time, realism has taken on various meanings, to include identification with the dark and gritty aspects of life. In *CENTERLINE*, however, the term refers to the accurate portrayal of flight operations, military medical care, combat operations, the concerns of wounded soldiers returning to a world that may not understand them, and families stretched to the limits by the trials of war and separation.

Repetition: Use of the same word, phrase or idea several times for emphasis or to draw attention. In *CENTERLINE* Chapter 9, the doors thump closed separating the chaplain from his failure to reach and help a suicidal soldier. In the next line, the landing gear thumps down on the runway, as the doors prepare to open, leaving him to face what he thinks will be his failure as a pastor at home.

Roundness: Not a standard literary term, but useful in

describing the cyclical nature of life as described in some literary works. When the student copilot of Chapter 2 becomes the experienced pilot of the Epilogue, a sort of roundness has been achieved in the story—sad and inspiring at the same time.

Simile: A direct comparison between two things, which uses *like* or *as*. It increases the emotional power of a passage by creating additional clarity, images, and feelings in readers' minds. In *CENTERLINE* Chapter 8, the pilot explains the evasive maneuvers he will perform upon departing the airport, and says he wants to cross the end of the runway "climbing like a bat out of hell." This simile is actually so common in the American vernacular of English that it is recognized as an idiom.

Style: The unique contribution of the author, combining *what* he/she has chosen to say, and *how* he/she has chosen to say it. The best way to identify an author's style is to ask after finishing a passage or chapter, "What impressed me most about what I just read and why?" The answer to that question should serve as the start point in describing the author's style. Conversely, a critic might ask "What annoys me about this book?" The answer is no doubt connected to the author's style.

Symbol: A real thing that also represents something else. A red light on the top of a police car is both a real thing (a light) and a representation of the authority of the state, telling people to stop or get out of the way. In *CENTERLINE* Chapter 11, the pendant the pilot gives his wife for Christmas is a double symbol. It is a real object—a gold pendant with jewels crafted to look like a beacon light for an airport. As the pilot explains, the beacon that the pendant represents is also a symbol of something else—the way to home and safety.

Theme: The overall subject or idea of the work. In a novel of substance, it will usually be expressed as a universal. The subtitle for the first edition of *CENTERLINE* was "War throws people off center. So does coming home." Might this be considered the theme of the novel? Does some other phrase work better?

Thesis: An argument for a solution to a problem. In a novel, the thesis is similar to a theme, but is offered if the text poses a problem rather than simply a statement. Some readers have suggested that the thesis of *CENTERLINE* is posed by the Ranger when he says, "everybody who went to war was shot . . . And everybody needs to recover." (page 128)

Tone: The attitude that the author establishes toward the readers, and their resulting attitude toward him/her. Exploring this term leads to broader questions: How do the readers respond to the author as a result of the tone? Is it formal? Confidential? Trusting? Skeptical? Professional? Antagonistic? Playful? Does the tone move the readers to trust the author? Enjoy him/her but for light subjects only? Embrace the author and his/her ideas? Craft different ideas instead?

Tone versus Mood: *CENTERLINE* is the story of four groups of people: returning wounded soldiers, flight crew, medical team, waiting families.

> » The attitude that the author engenders in the readers toward this subject matter is the *mood*.

> » The attitude that the author engenders in the readers toward the way the story is told is the *tone*.

Voice/Point of View: The vantage point from which the author presents the information. Some examples include:

> » **Omniscient:** The author presents all the information in a reliable manner from the outside, as though he knows the final resolution from the beginning of the story . . . as indeed he does (e.g., James Michener's *Hawaii*)
>
> » **Limited:** The author presents material from the perspective of one character as that character learns it, and with any limitations with which he/she is encumbered (e.g., the character might be a child with limited understanding, as in *To Kill a Mockingbird*).
>
> » **Unreliable:** The author presents the material from the perspective of a character telling a story that may or may not be true (e.g., the main character in the movie *The Usual Suspects*).

NOTE: This guide is written in the first person, from the point of view of an expert author and teacher. That is an unusual approach for an academic work. My special position allows me to use this unique point of view. Do you think it works?

GETTING IT: THREE QUESTIONS FOR GREATER UNDERSTANDING

The previous three sections of this guide described the:

» Concepts of literary criticism and analysis,
» Literary form and structure, and how they shape the meaning of a work, and
» Literary terms and tools used to analyze how the text influences readers.

These ideas may be examined by asking three basic questions. Together they form a framework useful in conducting an inquiry into the novel.

1 **What happened?** Do readers understand the events, thoughts, actions, etc. in the text?
2 **How did it happen?** How did the author manipulate the text to achieve the desired effects?

3   **What difference does it make?** How do the parts
    of the work tie together, and why should readers
    care about the text, techniques, and message of
    the book?

WHAT HAPPENED?

Literature teachers are frequently astonished at how many
students read a passage and simply do not understand what
happened. When teaching a novel, no further learning or
literary analysis can take place until this issue is resolved.
Here is a set of questions to use after each reading assignment to help students understand what happened.

»   **Context:** Where does the assigned section fall
    within the book? (Prologue? Beginning? Middle?
    End? Epilogue?) What does this tell readers to
    expect from the action? How does the content fit
    together with what students have already read?
    Based on this reading, what do readers expect to
    happen next?
»   **Who:** Which characters make an appearance in
    this reading assignment? Which do not?
»   **What:** What do the characters do? What is done
    to them? Who or what does it? Is this action
    intentional, accidental, or just "fate"?
»   **When:** When do the events, actions, and thoughts
    take place? What is the timeline of events within
    the reading assignment? All in the present? Is
    some part a flashback? Does some part jump for-
    ward into the future?

» **Where:** Where do the events take place?

» **How:** How do the characters act, think and speak? Externally? Internally?

» **Is there anything the reader did not understand?** Technical terms? Historical references? Issues with the setting?

HOW DID IT HAPPEN?

Once readers completely understand what transpired, they can go back and use the tools, terms, and techniques of literary analysis to figure out how the author manipulated the characters, setting, and actions to convey a message through the narrative as it unfolded. Why do this? To better enjoy the book (readers will be surprised at what they missed!), and gain a better perspective on life (which is what literature provides).

Here is a framework to use in working through this analysis. Not every point requires a comment for every chapter. Rather, once readers have completed the entire book, the analysis may be holistic, using this framework (tied to the definitions already provided) as a start point to examine individual passages or scenes, then comparing them with scenes before and after to see how the book works as a whole.

» Form
  › Autobiographical; Journey; Manners; Episodic; Realistic; Romance; Fantasy; Science Fiction; Specific Genre; High-tech; Historical; Action-Adventure; Other; Blended or Hybrid.

» Structure

› Conceit; Setting; Plot; Characters; Plot Development; Narrator

» Tools, Terms, and Techniques

Allusion	Hero	Novel	Roundness
Analysis	Imagery	Plot	Simile
Archetype	*In medias res*	Point of View	Style
Catharsis	Irony	Prologue	Symbol
Characterization	Metaphor	Protagonist	Theme
Dramatic Structure	Mood	Purpose	Thesis
Flashback	Narration	Realism	Tone
Foreshadowing	Narrative	Repetition	Voice

WHAT DIFFERENCE DOES IT MAKE?

This guide is intended to be used for *traditional literary analysis*, which includes how the following are reflected in individual passages, and in the overall shape and impact of the book:

» **Designing Author:** How does the author's design drive the action and message of a passage or a book?

» **Crafted Work:** How do selected literary techniques design/drive the action and message of a passage or a book?

» **Entertainment:** Not every passage of every book has some great, galactic meaning. It's okay for a book to be enjoyable.

» **Higher Order Meaning:** What important ideas may educated readers may take away from the book?

» **Self-Aware Readers:** What do readers contribute from the perspectives of Reason and Emotion, taken separately and taken together? Did the author anticipate and use the readers' perspective?

FOR CENTERLINE ONLY

AUTHOR'S NOTES

Each chapter analysis in Section 7 of this guide includes a final note where I speak directly to the readers about writing and revising *CENTERLINE*. I think this provides an interesting and unique perspective. But this is not a part of the suggested Three Questions for Greater Understanding and resulting framework(s) for traditional literary analysis, because the author is not usually available to provide first person commentary.

GETTING *CENTERLINE*: CHAPTER BY CHAPTER

Using previous sections in this guide, apply the terms, tools, and techniques to examine the novel *CENTERLINE* in detail.

ACKNOWLEDGMENTS AND FOREWORD

WHAT HAPPENED?

When reading a novel, many readers skip the Acknowledgments and the Foreword, preferring to get straight into the action of the prologue or the first chapter. This is generally a mistake, as the Acknowledgments allow the author to speak directly to the readers concerning how and why the book was written, and the Foreword usually allows some outside expert to put the book into a broader context. And so it is with *CENTERLINE*.

Two points should strike readers about this acknowledgments section.

The first is the author's heavy reliance on technical experts for scenes about flying, medical care, military family life, and the realities of life as a soldier recovering from wounds suffered in war.

The second striking point is the author's heavy reliance on friends and family to provide that expertise. There is an intensely personal story behind the details provided in this book.

Ignoring a Foreword can be an even greater reader error. In *CENTERLINE*, the Foreword is penned by the author's son, already mentioned as a technical advisor for the book concerning issues of ground combat, and a veteran of the war in Iraq. He tells us three things in very personal terms:

> » The war described in *CENTERLINE* really happened (the Foreword places it in time and space),
> » Now it is over, so this is a historical novel, and
> » The novel tells readers about a part of the history of the war that few people see or think about—damaged equipment and damaged people returned home for repair.

② HOW DID IT HAPPEN?

The Foreword tells readers something about the form of the book to follow, in a very clever way.

The setting for the Foreword is the end of the war in Iraq—in fact, the last day of that war. The story of the Foreword (the conceit) is a trip (a familiar literary technique frequently accompanied by growth and increased knowledge and self-awareness). This trip is by a military convoy moving along a route previously used to go to war. The convoy is returning from war, with the equipment (and people) battered and worn, yet still marked by military discipline and bearing. This is a story not previously told—of the used up implements of war, collected in marshaling yards (collection points), shipped home, and repaired to some extent, but never returned to the condition they enjoyed before the war.

Then the story turns (readers should always look for such turning points) from focus on the war-weary equipment to a focus on war-weary people.

> *And what about the men and women who rode in those vehicles? Those who slept on them, hid behind them, killed from them, and bled in them? They, after all, are the beating heart and quivering muscles of the military machine. What of the damage they sustained? Who tells about the hospitals, the psych wards, and the VA centers . . . And who tells of the heroes who evacuated the wounded—nursed their bodies and repaired their spirits . . . Who remembers them? (page xiv)*

The answer, according to the Foreword, is this novel. So readers see a double metaphor at work: the novel is like the Foreword, and the Foreword compares the trip of damaged equipment back for repair, to the trip of damaged people back for healing. Both the equipment and the people will be salvaged—but both will be marked forever by the scars of war.

This suggests that the theme of the book will be the difficulty of repairing people—of returning them to a well-centered life—after a trip to war.

The tone of the Foreword is sparse, factual, and to the point, like a military report. The mood is somber. The style is profoundly personal.

WHAT DIFFERENCE DOES IT MAKE?

Taken together, the Acknowledgements and Foreword tell readers several important things about what to expect of this novel:

» It will be rich in technical detail,
» Although placed in a historical frame, it will tell some universal truths about people and war,
» Readers can expect an intense emotional identification with the characters.

AUTHOR'S NOTES

Many times authors begin with the idea for a story and then research it. In the case of *CENTERLINE*, I began by researching stories from family and friends returned from the war, and turned them into an idea for this book.

Because this novel is largely about Air Force flying and missions, I relied mostly on my younger son (an Air Force pilot who has flown such missions) for expertise in describing the aircraft and flights. I turned to my older son (with Army expertise in Iraq) to pen the Foreword. I think I am pretty spare and direct as a writer. My older son's prose makes mine look flowery and verbose by comparison. I was completely unprepared for the Foreword he penned, which perfectly captured the theme of the book in a way that moved me to tears.

THE HERC AND MAP: WOLF 41/AIR EVAC 1492/AIRPORTS

WHAT HAPPENED?

The map shows all airport destinations included in the stateside missions and emergencies of Wolf 41 and Air Evac 1492. (As explained on page 37, the aircraft and crew change call signs when they are carrying wounded personnel.)

The Herc is a short, separate segment of the book providing historical facts about the aircraft that flies the missions: the C-130E transport. The segment notes that this model of aircraft has since retired from the inventory.

HOW DID IT HAPPEN?

The map accurately reflects real locations routinely visited by U.S. Air Force aeromedical evacuation units, or aircraft afflicted by in-flight emergencies.

The passage about the Hercules is entirely fact-based, but it places the story of the fictitious C-130E in *CENTERLINE* in the historic context of other missions worldwide over the previous 50 years. It also introduces the aircraft in a way that personalizes it, first by giving it a name (The Herc), and then by suggesting that it is an admirable character in its own right: "The C-130E that plays a stoic lead role in this book is a great aircraft that has grown weary in the service of its country" (page xviii).

The aircraft is described from an omniscient perspective, which suggests the independent reliability of a technical or historical report.

The last two sentences of the section tell the real story of a real aircraft, and then suggest that the archetypal C-130E thus brought to life, might relate the narrative of *CENTERLINE* as a story that really happened—thus cementing the impression of a novel based on historical fact.

③ WHAT DIFFERENCE DOES IT MAKE?

When perused quickly by readers eager to push on to start the story, The Herc and The Map seem like courtesies offered by the author to help set the story in time and place.

However, a more careful analysis shows the two segments work together to prepare readers for the setting (in the skies and at real locations in the United States), conceit (tired aircraft and tired crews doing their duties at the edge of their capabilities), characters (crews and aircraft "who have put duty above family, and service above self, day after day and night after night, in every kind of weather . . ." (page xviii), and plot (which, as it unfolds, seems quite plausible, after this historical background).

It also grants historical validation to readers' early emotional attachment to the characters to follow. Readers are prepared to like these "selfless servants" even before meeting them.

AUTHOR'S NOTES

The Map and The Herc were not part of the first edition of this work. They were added at the request of publisher (and experienced screenwriter) Jay Lavender, for the purposes outlined in (3) above. After having read the novel, do you think the additions are necessary? Did they work as intended?

PROLOGUE: IFE

WHAT HAPPENED?

Time and place matter: 1230 hours 22 December 2007: SR219, Arkansas

The Prologue (placed before the beginning of the trip that constitutes the plot of the book) opens with an unnamed character using nature (and hunting) to focus and center his life. This action on the ground is quickly superseded by the roar of massive transport aircraft flying low overhead, and readers are transported inside where they meet five crew members, and join a technically (and emotionally) intensive low-level—high-speed training mission inside a speeding C-130E aircraft. The time is set as during the Iraq war, but the location is a well-established training route in Arkansas. The aircraft is described as reliable but tired, and various possible maintenance problems are established. The crew is in danger even when doing routine training.

As images of mountains, trees, humans, and animals flash past the windows of the aircraft, the crew performs various intricate technical activities to prepare the ship (and three others following them) for a practice mission dropping simulated supplies to soldiers on the ground. During the airdrop, the crew demonstrates a combination of technical expertise and adaptability, and the pilot in particular shows a cool professionalism that seems more machinelike than human.

Immediately upon achieving a successful airdrop, the crew is notified by their least experienced crew member (an alarmed loadmaster, by himself in the rear of the aircraft) that the plane is filling with smoke. The more experienced crew members in the front of the aircraft take appropriate actions (described in technical detail), while the "new guy" in the rear makes several mistakes: picking up a fire extinguisher (not appropriate for an electrical fire), disconnecting his intercom to move back in the aircraft, and leaving his oxygen mask behind in the process. When he drops the fire extinguisher in an unsteady moment, it strikes the deck, and spins upward striking him in the head, destroying his intercom, and knocking him to the ground with a bleeding head wound.

Unable to contact the loadmaster and fearing the worst, the pilot dispatches the navigator to investigate. Although the loadmaster is not badly injured, he is bleeding profusely and the navigator reports his condition as "not good at all" (page 20). In a flashback, the pilot thinks of an incident in combat when wounded soldiers dying in the back of his aircraft were described with the same words. He decides to declare an "In Flight Emergency" (IFE), followed by diversion to a nearby civilian airfield.

This action is again described in technical detail, and again the crew performs smoothly, with the pilot showing exceptional professionalism. Once on the ground, when the navigator encourages the pilot to go easy on the new loadmaster and his "new guy mistake," the pilot's response is harsh and overly professional. "Trying is not good enough. This is all about doing the *right* thing, not just *something*," he barks (page 24).

As the copilot departs the airfield taking the loadmaster to be checked for his injuries, he notes that the pilot's hyperprofessionalism has paid off—the aircraft and crew have returned safely and are parked exactly on the centerline of the taxiway.

❷ HOW DID IT HAPPEN?

The book is set just after noon (1230 hours in military time), three days before Christmas in 2007. Apparently the author has a purpose for selecting such a specific time and place. Readers should look for that purpose.

Remember that a prologue is intended to introduce important elements of the story early so that the narrative is not interrupted later to explain those details. Launching into the story *in medias res* establishes the book as an action-adventure narrative, and the detailed description of flying action tells readers to be ready for a high-tech tale. The images are arresting, but they flash by the windows, suggesting the mission as an imperative that leaves no time for reflection. The description of a tired old aircraft (and a tired crew) "hauling the water" (note the metaphor) while others are at war, establishes the historical frame and sets the stage for crew stress and maintenance problems later in the book. The pilot's flashback to a previous crisis when he was at war establishes his mental state, suggesting that despite his own professionalism and high standards for others, he may be carrying some mental "baggage" from previous events.

The one important part of the novel's form *not* established in the Prologue is the readers' emotional attachment to the characters. Instead, the entire passage suggests a machine-like emotional detachment from the crew, and especially from the pilot. The narrator's voice is like that of a crew member on the intercom—flat, clipped, precise, and minimal. From the inside, flying is not romantic; it is a deadly serious business that takes full concentration without distractions. Later it will appear that this means without the distractions from family as well.

Also, the conceit of the story is *not* established in this chapter. The Prologue "starts the clock" on the three-day timeline of the story, establishing another reason for the wife's unhappiness with her husband (the pilot) in Chapter 1. (See the next section: having just finished this mission, the pilot did not have to take another one so close to Christmas.) The mission in the Prologue is not a part of the mission that makes up the central narrative of the book. This flight is a separate event. It establishes the setting, and indeed foreshadows some of the key themes and events of the book. It is not part of plot development. Instead, it establishes a context that imparts meaning to the Epilogue, and drives home the theme of the book.

The title—IFE, later explained to mean In Flight Emergency—has a double meaning. There is an IFE in the aircraft (smoke and an injured crew man) and an IFE in the mind of the pilot (flashback to wounded soldiers dying in the back of his aircraft). This technique of "double meaning" is used with every chapter title in the book.

WHAT DIFFERENCE DOES IT MAKE?

The Prologue establishes an essential background in many areas (characterization, technology, flight procedures, historical setting, etc.) thus allowing the story to rush forward without interruption once it starts.

Along with the section on The Herc, the Prologue connects the story backward in time. The Epilogue (at the end of the book) connects the story forward. Thus, the central narrative described in Chapters 1–11 is both specific to a particular time and place, and also part of a much larger story about the military, service, and loss. It happens at Christmas 2007. It has happened before. It will happen again.

Also, note the abrupt transition on page 15 from the end of the airdrop mission to the beginning of the In Flight Emergency. There is no place for readers to pause between these two major parts of the chapter. Many readers have said of the book, "I couldn't put it down." That effect is created by stylistic design. In many places in the book, actions bleed together, the next beginning before the first is quite done. The result is a sense of rushing momentum that pulls readers forward.

AUTHOR'S NOTES

What is the function of the first three pages of the Prologue? The vignette of a hunter interrupted by a flight of aircraft low overhead is unlike anything else in the book. Why include it? And what of the hunter, who never appears again?

In my mind as author, the hunter represents the readers—searching for meaning, trying to use nature and the implements of man to center a restless mind. He observes this compelling image (the story of *CENTER-LINE*) passing close by, and is drawn in. Before you know it, the perspective shifts to inside the aircraft, and away we go. Note that the aircraft's wing-wave at the end of the third page is repeated in the last paragraph of the book, establishing roundness with The Epilogue that suggests the cycle goes on.

A final note: In an early draft I specified that the load-master was knocked unconscious by the fire extinguisher. My technical advisors informed me that such a blow would require that he be taken off flight status—perhaps forever. After careful research, I modified the scene to specify that he received a superficial cut that bled heavily—but the force of the blow hit the headset and not the head. Technical research is important when you are writing a high-tech adventure story for people who really know the subject matter.

CHAPTER 1: STORM WARNING

🔘 **WHAT HAPPENED?**

Time and place matter: 1930 hours 22 December: Little Rock Air Force Base (AFB), Arkansas.

Later the same day as the Prologue, at the pilot's home.

This is the beginning of the narrative that comprises the book.

In Chapter 1, we follow the pilot home, meet his wife, and discover a deep conflict over the amount of time he is devoting to military missions at the expense of his family.

The chapter opens with the security routine required to enter a military base. It follows the pilot through a military housing area of identical homes, and through the snow, down the centerline of the street, to the only dark house on the block—the only one without Christmas lights in preparation for the holiday, three days away.

In the kitchen, the pilot finds a cool reception from a wife who can recite the number of days he has been away from home in the last three years. She presses home the point that his absences leave the family unprepared for the holiday. When she learns that he has volunteered for a mission that might mean another missed Christmas (a mission flying wounded soldiers home for the holidays), she is incensed. She asks: "The gifts aren't bought. The tree's not up. You missed the preschool party and the kindergarten party. Your kids are the only ones on this block who don't have lights on their house. And you volunteered to leave again? . . . Don't you love us?" (page 32).

While the pilot-husband stands a conflicted mute, unable to articulate the source of his inner conflict between duty to family and duty to mission, the wife lays out her core complaint. Her husband will no longer communicate about what he has seen and done; he won't talk about what he thinks and feels. When she asks, "Is there something you need to talk about?" he takes the comment as a recommendation that he see a psychiatrist. Sensitive that charges of Post Traumatic Stress Disorder (PTSD) might end his career, he overreacts, and then is concerned that his overreaction might make matters worse.

As the chapter ends, she is unaware of the deep schism she has opened. He has begun to build a mental and emotional wall to keep out his own wife. He walks away and she lets him go. He enters the bedroom, turns out the light, and sleeps alone—preparing for the beginning of the trip that starts in Chapter 2.

HOW DID IT HAPPEN?

In the Prologue, readers met a pilot so mechanically super-proficient that "It was almost scary" (page 25). On the next page (page 26, the opening of Chapter 1) we see that his life demands multiple roles: "Captain-pilot-husband-father." As the conflict develops in the family kitchen, the pilot is unable to transition from military proficiency to human warmth, even with a wife who loves him and wants his company. The historical, high-tech, adventure aspects of the story disappear, and readers find themselves in the midst of a timeless tale about a soldier torn between duty to family and mission, and a wife defending her home against forces she cannot understand.

Readers sense that something is wrong—they feel a

bit of foreshadowing here. There is something below the surface that the pilot needs to share but won't. Readers are offered no flashback or hint of the underlying problem. There are no references or literary insights to explain the tension. The origin of the problem is a mystery (and will remain so until the next-to-last chapter of the book). Readers simply see two good people who apparently love each other but cannot communicate about something that is tearing their marriage apart.

Following the pattern set in the Prologue, the subtitle of Chapter 1 ("Storm Warning") has a double meaning. Certainly the pilot drives home through a snow storm that, according to the last paragraph of the chapter, might get better or worse. But the same may also be said of the "storm" between husband and wife: it might get better or it might get worse. At this point in the story, it is hard to tell.

Also, in this chapter the double meaning of the term "centerline" becomes evident. Certainly it is a technical aviation term referring to the dashed white line that runs down the center of a runway, or the yellow line that runs down the center of a taxiway (see the cover). In this chapter, it is also the line running down the center of the street that leads the pilot through the storm to home. It is this centerline that is obscured by snow from the storm at the end of Chapter 1. And the wife says to the pilot, "You have no balance in your life, Mike. No center. We're supposed to do that for you. We are supposed to be the center. And you won't let us." Clearly, the pilot can land his plane on the centerline of the runway, but he cannot find the centerline of his life. The narrative has begun.

WHAT DIFFERENCE DOES IT MAKE?

Many readers will not make this connection until the final two chapters, but this novel about wounded warriors coming home begins by showing the life of a wounded warrior (the pilot) at home. His wounds are invisible, but serious nonetheless. As readers will learn in Chapters 10 and 11, these wounds are the result of a mistake he made while flying a load of wounded to a hospital in Iraq. His mistakes as command pilot resulted in further injuries, and he carries that load of guilt on every mission, unable to talk to anyone about it. Seeking to atone for his mistake and return to the centerline of his life, he takes every mission available, and trains new pilots to a standard of perfection he did not seek until after he made his mistakes. No doubt he is being too hard on himself. Until he talks to someone (like his wife) about the issue, no one can reassure him and help him recover.

As the narrative progresses, returning through the storm to the centerline denotes both returning to the safety of the airport, and returning to a happy and balanced life. Ultimately, returning to the centerline becomes the goal of almost all the characters in the book.

For the wife's part, see the subtitle of the book: "Not Every Hero Is at the Front." Her fight has been on the home front, trying to run the house, raise two children, and maintain a home for a husband who can't help and can't explain why.

If a teacher discusses this chapter with students who are just starting the book, they will have only a faint sense that something they can't see is going on behind the scenes.

Once they have finished the book, they will be able to both see and feel how this chapter sets the background and the direction for the entire novel.

AUTHOR'S NOTES

After I finished an early draft of the book, I asked several former and current military wives to read it. They liked everything about the book except for the character of the wife, whom they disliked intensely. "I moved the whole house halfway around the world by myself, with my husband deployed and two kids with the chicken pox," one military spouse said. "And she's upset that he is late for dinner. She needs to grow up!"

Of course, my intent was to make her a sympathetic character to emphasize the burden that a long war places on military families. To accomplish that, I had to redraft the chapter and her character. Can you guess what changes I made?

CHAPTER 2: LUCKY FEW

WHAT HAPPENED?

Time and place matter: 0500 hours 23 December: Little Rock AFB to Scott AFB, Illinois.

Chapter 2 is the beginning of the trip that constitutes the central narrative of the book.

After tracking the crew's travel to Scott Air Force Base (where air evac missions originate), and noting the change of call signs from Wolf 41 to Air Evac 1492, the scene switches first to a briefing room, and then inside the aircraft, as readers are introduced to myriad technical skills and requirements involved with a mission like the one in *CENTERLINE*. The essential aspects of planning for a flight, and planning for the medical support of wounded in flight, are laid out in detail, but at a pace that keeps the crew (and the readers) moving and focused on the mission. This approach is repeated throughout the book—the requirements are challenging, but there is only time to accomplish them, not ponder them. This, of course, is a problem for all concerned—they know how to function, but not how to live with the memory of some of their failed functions in the past.

The same briefings serve to introduce the medical team, a new copilot, and a reporter who will cover the story of this homecoming for the press. The medical team includes a doctor, but (much to his bemusement) the strongest personality on the team seems to be an experienced flight nurse who echoes the hyperprofessionalism of the pilot. In fact, the two "alpha dog" personalities clash at first. Once on the aircraft and into the mission, each recognizes and respects the competence of the other, so they work well together. As the mission progresses, however, it becomes clear through flashbacks that they also share an inability to come to grips with issues from their past.

The young copilot (different from the experienced staff officer copilot introduced in the Prologue) is recently arrived in the unit and still learning. The command pilot both trains and evaluates her during all phases of the trip. The pressure from such oversight is heavy.

Also introduced in the briefings, and as the crew loads the aircraft, is a reporter from a local newspaper who is seeking a "feel good" story about the mission of returning wounded home at Christmas.

The wounded who are loaded into the aircraft for the trip home are tenuous, isolated individuals. They move with determination and courage, but are all apprehensive about the end of their trip, where they will face family and the reality of a life forever changed. They understand that they are a "Lucky Few" (the title of the chapter) to be coming home, but they remain apprehensive none the less.

Passenger loading is interrupted by a Ranger who has lost both legs but refuses to be carried on board the aircraft or ride in the aircraft on a litter (military stretcher). The response of the Ranger, fighting against the helplessness imposed by his wounds, and the impersonal discipline of the medical care and safety measures, creates an immediate conflict with the head nurse/Medical Crew Director (MCD). The crisis is averted for the moment through the Ranger's show of strength and determination, which even the nurse must grudgingly respect.

Flight preparations pause (breaking the rapid progression of the loading and the story) for two patients on litters. One is seriously (and recently) injured, and the other has suffered psychological wounds that require him to be sedated and strapped to his litter.

For several pages the author follows and explains the technical complexity of engine start and take off. At the last moment, the pilot switches responsibility for the aircraft to the copilot—and the narrative of the mission is interrupted by the copilot's flashback to humiliation before her father and a high school basketball crowd when she failed to seize the initiative and lead. Resolved not to make that mistake again, she takes control of the aircraft and departs on the mission, pleased with her performance, and feeling "one of the lucky few" to be in the Air Force, on the aircraft, and in control.

The pilot is not so pleased.

② HOW DID IT HAPPEN?

Just as Chapter 1 set the background for a romantic story, Chapter 2 sets audience expectations for a high-tech action-adventure story, within a specific historical framework. In terms of dramatic structure, it completes the introduction (which begins with the Prologue). With the takeoff of Air Evac 1492, the rising action (no pun intended) begins.

Note how early in the morning the flight crew begins work. For safety, crews may only fly for a limited number of hours before they are required to rest. We will see later that this becomes a limiting factor, threatening their ability to get home for Christmas.

The briefing at Scott serves a triple purpose—it continues to set a clipped, technical, and realistic tone for the book; it begins to establish the actions and motivations of individual characters; and it explains the mission that comprises the core of the book. (Compare the briefing with the map on page xx.)

As the wounded begin to arrive at the aircraft, the author steps out of the story and provides an extended description and analysis of the system (and the people) who care for the wounded and move them from the battlefield, through treatment and recovery, to home. This is a risky move from a literary perspective. A change in voice can disrupt the flow of the story to the point that the narrative is never properly reestablished. However, the author thought that the information provided is so interesting and so compelling that the overall story is enhanced, and readers will stay engaged through this short interruption. In other words, the emotional payoff is worth the literary risk.

The clash between the nurse and the Ranger provides a certain dramatic irony, because to some degree they are both right. Loading the wounded soldier and his new artificial legs on a litter is safer; letting him load by wheelchair and sit in a seat like others provides essential dignity to a man struggling to recover his sense of worth and independence. Clearly this clash of visions is not over.

The physical description of the wounded individuals continues the author's intentional parallel with Chaucer's *The Canterbury Tales*. In later chapters (as the pilgrimage continues), readers will hear what the characters say, then see what they really think in their "internal tales." In some cases, the imagery and conversation will reinforce readers' initial impressions. In other cases, readers will sense a dramatic irony between perception and reality.

This reality is reinforced unexpectedly when readers discover through dialogue that one of the patients strapped to a stretcher is afflicted not with physical wounds but by psychological damage. The fact that he is both sedated and accompanied by an armed guard to protect others should he become violent introduces a stark, realistic fact of war that stops the action momentarily while the crew (and the reader) ponder this hidden cost.

The technical aspect of the story is emphasized again by the detailed description of the medical team settling in the passengers for the flight, in the crew dynamics preparing for takeoff, and by the realism interjected by the business-like radio traffic between pilot and controllers. The technical aspects of the "crew brief" will become important in the plot's later critique of the copilot's performance.

Of course, the copilot's flashback to a moment of failure, coupled with her feeling of exultation at being in charge of an aircraft and a mission and a crew, establish her internal motivation for being in the Air Force, and for trying so hard to satisfy the command pilot's demands for professional perfection.

WHAT DIFFERENCE DOES IT MAKE?

This guide has already established that *CENTERLINE* is a hybrid of high-tech, action-adventure, historical, and romantic (emotional) engagement. This chapter completes locking that framework into place and launches the "pilgrimage" on its way.

In the Prologue, readers see action and technical challenges involved in tactical Air Force flying. In Chapter 1 the book is grounded in a specific historical moment, and readers see the emotional impact of war and service on the pilot and his family. In Chapter 2:

» The narrator/author steps out of his normal voice to show that this is a fictional version of a real (historical) mission, and fictional (amalgamated) versions of real people.

» The change of call sign to Air Evac 1492 establishes a connection to a well-known adventure trip (the voyage of Columbus to a new world).

» The actions of the flight crew and medical team reinforce the technical nature of the story—but suggest that there are humans with hopes and fears behind the military facades.

» The wounded are introduced more as caricatures than as characters—almost as props to justify the trip undertaken by the major characters. This will change later as readers learn that each has a very human, very personal "inside" story.

With the final technical sequence culminating in the takeoff, tension, pace, and momentum build, and all aspects of the story are coiled like a spring, awaiting release. Readers are ready to be launched on the mission.

Finally, note how the repetition of terms is used to establish thematic connections between various parts of the book. For example, on one hand stress within the pilot's family is the crux of the conflict in Chapter 1, and the copilot's memories of her own father/family are a source of distress in Chapter 2. On the other hand, the pilot talks about flying the wounded home as "taking care of our own," (page 31) and the author calls the teams and crews who care for and return the wounded home a "lucky few" because they are taking care of "family" (page 46). Many of the wounded will be met at the airport by supportive family. Some will not. In the Epilogue, the aircrew speeds to pick up wounded because "somebody in the family needed help" (page 275). Clearly the theme of family, and the conflict of loyalties between types of families, is a major theme in the book.

Also note (again) that the chapter title resonates in three different ways. The wounded going home are a "Lucky Few," as are the members of the "military family" who serve them. At the end of the chapter, the copilot is one of a lucky few doing a job she loves.

AUTHOR'S NOTES

I worked hard to avoid making the reporter a flat character who just served to ask questions for the readers. I rewrote her part several times to add depth and complexity so that her story would also provide some interest and surprises.

Technical passages are common in books related to military subjects. Engine start and take off is an unusually mundane subject for such a detailed description. I selected this approach for several reasons.

» First, it establishes my legitimacy with knowledge-able readers.

» It also demonstrates the complexity of military aviation to novice readers. It shows the difficulty of the basic tasks the copilot is trying to master. This understanding forms a backdrop later when the flying becomes a challenge.

» It feeds the perception of the pilot as hyperpro-fessional, capable of flawless execution of these complex tasks—yet struggling with the basics of human interaction with his wife.

I chose to stress the high-tech nature of flying (and later, of medical care) not just to entertain the readers, but to show that even those who master war professionally can be wounded by it emotionally.

CHAPTER 3: NOTHING TO REPORT

① WHAT HAPPENED?

Time and place matter: 0955 hours 23 December: Scott AFB to El Paso International Airport, Texas

The aircraft and crew are barely launched on their mission before the nurse rises to begin her technical routine. She has barely started before she is startled into a flashback to a horrible experience while treating another soldier earlier in her career. This is the first of many passages where an event of the moment will catapult the character (and the readers) into a traumatic situation from the past, which the character then buries in order to return to the routines of the day. Readers cannot so easily leave the traumatic images behind.

This brief event is followed by another quick scene where the reporter (and reader) are compelled to watch the private challenge of a wounded soldier who cannot negotiate the small toilet on the plane, and must stand in the aisle to urinate in a bottle with the help of a medical technician, while others look away. This indignity is followed rapidly by the pilot's criticism of the copilot's flying up front, the nurse's return to precise medical routine in the back, and another flashback to a time she apparently wants to forget—five distinct scenes and character interactions in six short pages.

The author interrupts briefly to explain a bit about the reporter's background and motivation, as well as her approach to writing. It involves gathering details from the lives of subjects, and then tailoring them into interesting stories that will engage readers and advance her career, even if they bear only passing resemblance to reality. This is clearly her intent for the story on the homecoming of wounded warriors, as she moves from seat to seat seeking the details she needs to spin a tale. Three times in a row she finds the intended subjects of those tales polite but distant, reluctant to share the details of their experiences, and insistent that she talk to others who are more interesting or more badly injured. Meanwhile, in each case, the interviewee flashes back to a painful and dramatic part of his or her personal story, which they keep locked inside and refuse to share. These characters include:

» An infantry lieutenant who carries the burden of knowing that his older brother went to prison for a crime that he committed (in self-defense), as well as the knowledge of his own capacity for explosive violence.

» A female mechanic, newly married and part of a family that highly values children, who knows her own wounds will leave her childless.

» A scout traumatized not so much by his lost leg as by his children's emotional response to that loss.

After a brief exchange where the pilot judges the copilot's performance harshly (and the technical challenge of flying is reinforced), the aircraft lands in El Paso, and some of the wounded are met by family. A fourth wounded soldier is introduced briefly as he departs alone, and another new character, a chaplain, attempts to explain to the reporter what the returning wounded are thinking and feeling. Without an understanding of the inner turmoil of the homecoming, she misses the real stories. The reporter is left with nothing to report.

② HOW DID IT HAPPEN?

As the trip that is the core of the narrative story for this book begins with a rush in this chapter, three things happen by literary design.

First, readers are exposed to multiple characters and situations in quick succession. Each scene reflects one of three approaches:

» Technical competence, as with in-flight procedures, the complex chorography of landing, and the assessment and care of each patient according to their individual charts;

» A bland, shallow story, as wounded relate the skeletal outline of their situation to the reporter, accompanied by some version of "Everybody here is worse off than me" (page 82);

» Compelling emotional detail, marked by vibrant images, as the wounded think back to the violence of war, or the change in relations with their families that their wounds will bring.

Note that throughout the chapter, current action is confined to the interior of an aircraft—frequently to a single seat in the aircraft—and to the airport in El Paso. In the flashbacks, the action ranges broadly—from combat in Iraq, to an emergency room in Germany, to a hospital in Washington, DC. This produces a sense that the actors are trapped in the aircraft on a trip they do not control, further helping readers identify and emotionally engage with them.

Second, there is little or no transition between these events. Note, for example, the way the scout's tearful concern about meeting his children as an amputee, tails directly into a flight sequence on page 85:

> He raised his hands and covered his eyes. And he wept again.
> "I think that rpm gauge is fluctuating again." The engineer reached forward to tap it.

The stylistic technique of cramming scenes together like this produces the sense that events are rushing forward (like the aircraft) with no way to stop them.

Third, several important ideas are planted in this chapter, foreshadowing future events and themes.

- » One is from the pilot who critiques the copilot's short comings with, "Don't try. Do" (page 64). This is a variation on his criticism of the loadmaster in the Prologue: "Trying is not good enough" (page 24). And a repeat of his wife's criticism of his own attempts to be a better husband and father: "Trying is not enough. You need to do it right" (page 35). An alert reader will expect to see this theme again later in the book.
- » The idea that at one point in the past the nurse had wanted to remember everything, while now she depends on work to help her forget, suggests a deeper story to come.
- » The scout's comment that "Everyone here has been wounded . . . I just don't have much to talk about," is soon to be echoed by other wounded.
- » The failure of an rpm gauge (again) will take on additional importance later on.

⊙ WHAT DIFFERENCE DOES IT MAKE?

The point to be made here is that the vibrant images and dramatic action of the flashbacks are contrasted against the mundane if technically complex actions of the moment, to show that much more is going on in the memories of the veterans than the trip itself would suggest. Meanwhile, events rush forward, dragging all the characters toward an uncertain future. The result is an unusual combination of plot action and inaction, while readers become attached to the characters.

Note that the character flashbacks are brief. These passages do not transform the characters into fully rounded figures. They do make them intensely human—vulnerable—in a way that strikes an emotional chord with readers.

Their uniform refusal to talk about their experiences suggests something unhappy is going on inside. There is an admirable aspect of self-denial in their repeated suggestions that others have been hurt worse and have better stories. There is also a disquieting aspect to that denial. Being wounded was a major event in their lives, and refusal to talk about it does not bode well for their psychological health.

This all creates a repetitive dramatic irony between what characters are saying and what readers know they are thinking and feeling. Readers are in on the conceit. The reporter is not. She is trying to spin a happy story of homecoming—but she can't. Readers know the truth—homecomings are bittersweet at best, and some are not sweet at all.

All this sets up the readers and the story for a dramatic reveal about the pilot's experience, forthcoming in Chapters 10 and 11.

What is all this moving toward? Based on the Prologue and first three chapters of the book, how can readers describe the direction of the narrative? The chaplain, a veteran of both combat and multiple homecomings, makes the key connection as he explains to the reporter that when the wounded arrive home their roles change, and they no longer know who they are. They are trying "to get their balance" he says. They are trying to get back to the centerline in their lives.

AUTHOR'S NOTES

Some readers have asked, "Why is the pilot so hard on the new copilot?" Actually this is a traditional and very realistic relationship. New pilots arrive in their units with basic flying skills, but missing essential experience. Pairing them with a gruff experienced vet to show them the ropes, and hold them accountable, is a very effective training technique.

Foreshadowing is an excellent technique to encourage close and engaged reading. Once readers catch onto the fact that the author is dropping clues to future events along the way, they can begin to actively search for little mysteries in every scene. Writing these clues is best done in reverse—by deciding on the effect you want to achieve and where you want to achieve it, and then reaching back to previous chapters to plant appropriate clues.

For example, I wanted to show that there are many types of pain in war, so I decided early that a personal betrayal by a love gone bad would be a logical cause for the nurse's retreat from reality into professionalism. In outlining the book, I saw an opportunity to pair the revelation of her betrayal with that of the Ranger by his fiancée at the culmination of his pilgrimage to Garden City (Chapter 8). Then I selected places in previous chapters where I could begin to suggest some hidden reason that she now preferred work to friendships. Sometimes I included a revealing flashback (see page 66); sometimes just a suggestive sentence ("She had a lot that she wanted to forget" also page 66).

Concerning the title of the chapter: "Report" is a military term. It suggests a formal recitation of facts—the truth. Ask yourself, in this chapter, who has nothing to report? The answer is the reporter—the person whose job it is to report. I was consciously trying to re-create the ironic effect at the end of *All Quiet on the Western Front* by Eric Remarque. There, after years of suffering on the German Western Front in World War I, the main character is killed during a lull in the action. It is a horrible tragedy that affects readers profoundly. Yet because the day was not marked by significant military activity, the formal Army report for the day notes "All quiet on the Western Front."

I was seeking to achieve a similar ironic impact. In this chapter, readers see the drama of many fellow humans struggling with wounds, changed lives, and internal emotions. The reporter, an observer without access to the flashbacks, sees nothing to report.

CHAPTER 4: BROKEN

WHAT HAPPENED?

Time and place matter: 1305 hours 23 December: El Paso, Texas

As the wounded passengers destined for El Paso meet their families and depart, the crew turns to the problem of a broken gauge that will delay their departure until a replacement part is located and installed. Having noted another C-130 aircraft parked at the airport, the pilot dispatches the flight engineer with a bottle of expensive whisky in the hopes of enticing the other crew into providing the parts and expertise needed to fix the problem.

On the flight deck, the pilot turns to a critique of the new copilot's performance during the flight. Critiques of new pilots by instructor-pilots are notoriously brutal in the Air Force (as a way of driving home important points), but this review is more clinical in its logic—and stinging in its precision and correctness. Small errors with potentially large consequences are pointed out, like the maintenance of climb rates and departure speeds, and proper preparation for the final approach and landing. The copilot finds the public review humiliating.

The discussion is interrupted by the arrival of a new character—a restaurant owner and American Legion member who looks and acts like Santa Claus in an aloha shirt. A frequent "meeter and greeter" of wounded warriors passing through El Paso airport, he invites the passengers and crew to lunch while the aircraft is repaired. After clearing the idea with the medical team, he leads all except a skeleton crew (left to fix the gauge) to a waiting bus, and they depart to the restaurant. The passengers go willingly, but they are a sad and dispirited lot, as they consider their future lives and the changes that await them at home.

En route they pass an automobile accident where a car on fire reminds each soldier of some horrible event he or she witnessed in war, further dampening spirits.

Also during the trip, the reporter flirts with the navigator, hoping to create from his Air Force experiences a story she can sell to her editor. She is surprised (as is the copilot) to hear a poignant tale of escaping from Saigon as a child, growing up with adoptive parents on a Texas farm, serving in the Air Force, and enlisting for a second time after 9/11. It is an interesting, moving and highly personal story. The navigator, however, also declines a write-up, and points the reporter back to the recovering wounded instead.

Upon arrival at their destination, the wounded passengers, flight crew members, and medical staff discover that "Santa" owns a HOOTERS—a chain restaurant known for its scantily clad waitresses. Although the women on the bus might be expected to have some reservations about events to follow, the male visitors are strangely withdrawn as well, and it is a "sad little parade" that makes its way inside. The wounded are all thinking about how their wounds will change their lives, and whether they will be accepted after the loss they have suffered. The wounded Ranger springs into action (as best one can do from a wheelchair), and raises everyone's spirits with a show of enthusiasm, and military bearing.

Once inside, the reporter is surprised to find the civilian patrons more focused on the food than the waitresses. Still hoping to develop a story for her editor, she moves to a table where three amputees challenge her to be shocked at their prosthetic limbs. She retains her composure, is accepted into their "club," and joins their table.

The Ranger has a short talk with the waitresses about how to interact with the wounded by looking past their wounds and engaging them personally, eye to eye, as if with a friend.

Meanwhile back in Little Rock, the pilot's wife struggles with the challenges of running a family alone—buying groceries for Christmas dinner, managing children in the cold rain of a parking lot, and dealing with a car that won't start. She repeatedly attempts to engage her husband, but he takes her text messages for nagging, and refuses to respond. The chasm between them deepens.

HOW DID IT HAPPEN?

This chapter begins with a demonstration of the technical complexity of flying. In Chapter 3 (page 64) the pilot criticized the copilot's take-off for being too "by the book." In Chapter 4 he criticizes her for not knowing "the book" well enough, and thus missing key preparations during the flight. Once on the ground, he explains in detail the complex adjustments a pilot must make in landing. Together these passages use the premise of critiquing copilot performance to reinforce to readers the high-tech nature of flying, and of the novel.

Then the story shifts to an unusual dramatic structure—a rapid series of vignettes, each flowing into the next, reinforcing the emotional nature of the setting and readers' engagement with various characters. It becomes apparent that the narrative is being stitched together by multiple plot lines involving multiple characters. The pilot and his wife, the copilot, the reporter, the Ranger, the nurse, and some of the other wounded begin to gain depth and audience empathy as details of their past lives and current dilemmas unfold. The pilot and his wife can't talk, the copilot can't achieve the perfection she seeks, the navigator is hiding a dramatic life story behind a light-hearted exterior, the reporter continues to fail at getting a story for her editor, the Ranger throws himself into leadership when others falter, and the nurse runs a professional risk to provide the wounded a healing outside the range of her medical powers. The list goes on. Flat characters come alive because of small details that make them seem human—and vulnerable. The narrative and theme emerge *not* as a linear story of a main character, but as tapestry involving many characters, with each becoming more complete and lifelike as the details of their personal challenges stack up.

Note the repeated allusions to Santa and *The Night before Christmas.*

- » " . . . laying a finger aside his nose" (page 99),
- » "'Well, Donner and Blitzen!' the navigator exclaimed." (page 99),
- » "An elf!" (page 100),
- » "Like the down of a thistle, they were off" (page 102).

These literary references reinforce the timing of the story overall. It is Christmastime, and what should be a joyous pilgrimage home is actually a nerve-wracking voyage into a frightening future.

As the bus passes a traffic accident, notice how the imagery of the burning car reflected in the bus windows combines with flashbacks for each wounded character, to create an unspoken metaphor for the psychological trap of war. "'Get out!' their minds screamed. But nobody got out. Nobody ever got out" (page 103).

Note the powerful reference to another work of literature when the Ranger calls the nurse "Nurse Ratched" (page 109). The reference is to the over controlling villain-nurse of a psychiatric hospital in Ken Kesey's 1962 novel, *One Flew Over the Cuckoo's Nest*. Although delivered by the Ranger in a light tone as a backhanded compliment, the comparison is a stinging one, especially given the nurse's propensity to over control. The Ranger's withdrawal of this charge will later mark a turning point in their relationship (page 145).

Repetition of the tenuous and fragile emotional condition of the wounded is used several times in this chapter to establish and reinforce a mood that is somber, hesitant, and uncertain. They limp and lean on each other, then take seats by themselves as they load the bus. They are unusually quiet on the ride. They show trepidation as they unload at the restaurant, and crowd uncertainly around the door.

Toward the end of the chapter when the scene shifts abruptly to the pilot's wife back in Little Rock, the audience watches from an omniscient perspective her struggle to prepare a pleasant homecoming and Christmas dinner for her family. Awareness of the pilot's different perspective (he sees her expressions of interest and support as nagging) provides a dramatic irony that builds the tension and sense of foreboding about the destinies of these and other characters.

③ WHAT DIFFERENCE DOES IT MAKE?

Sitting broken on the side of the runway, its pilgrimage to Christmas, home, and security interrupted, waiting for someone else to provide the repairs essential for continued flight, The Herc provides a powerful metaphor for the men and women in this story. Struggling to fulfill its mission, but tired and worn from the rigors of service, it simply cannot heal itself. It needs outside help.

The wounded soldiers, and the flight and medical crews who move them, need help as well. They need someone to break the mood of sad resignation—to reinvigorate the spirit of hope and Christmas—to look past their wounds and "see the person inside" (page 114).

At the end of the chapter they are all still "broken," but there is a glimmer of hope on the horizon. The aircraft is being repaired, and the Ranger is preparing a group of attractive waitresses to restore the self-confidence the veterans need.

Additionally, several seeds are planted in this chapter that will grow to direct the individual stories later on.

» The copilot learns that the pilot's intense criticism indicates a confidence that she is capable of greater things.

» The nurse displays an understanding of the balance required between rigid enforcement of the rules, and the human touch sometimes essential for healing.

» The Ranger demonstrates a grudging admiration for the leadership shown by the nurse he had previously dismissed as hopelessly rule-bound.

» The doctor complains of stiffness in his knees.

» A malingering soldier, pretending to be hurt worse than he is, limps on the wrong leg.

» The reporter discovers a soldier with similar interests and a wit equal to her own.

» The pilot reinforces the pattern of cutting off communication with his wife.

This is not exactly foreshadowing—none of these details suggests a possible outcome in the future. But at some point in future chapters, each seemingly minor point will contribute to the further development of that character's story in an important way.

Also note that in what might otherwise be a melancholy and even depressing chapter, the restaurant owner who personifies Santa (in both appearance and generosity) provides balance and a bit of comic relief. The description and dialogue of this character are carefully crafted by the author. Too light a touch and the emotional optimism of the character might seem shallow. Too heavy a portrayal, and the message could be preachy and artificial.

AUTHOR'S NOTES

In the thirty-four years that I was in the military, I never saw a person on duty drink alcohol. Drinking alcohol is absolutely forbidden to the crews on Air Force aircraft. I did however see expensive liquor used as an enticement to get special help on maintenance or other problems on many occasions. So the idea of using alcohol to "lubricate" the situation on page 95 is absolutely realistic.

Many (perhaps most) of the flights carrying wounded home within the United States were (are) flown by Air National Guard Crews. Part of the theme of this story is the stress on families and crews of multiple deployments to wars that last for years, so I built the story around an active duty Air Force crew from Little Rock, the largest C-130 base in the world. Specifying that the crew flying a similar mission and providing assistance to repair Air Evac 1492 was from the Texas National Guard was my way of paying tribute to the citizen-soldiers and their families who also suffered through the stress of the wars in Iraq and Afghanistan.

Specifying that "Santa" and his "elf" were from the American Legion and the VFW respectively was also a way to provide an author's "tip of the hat" to these organizations and their members who provided support to returning veterans tirelessly for years.

Including the new copilot and her instructor's critique was originally an author's device to help explain the technical challenges of flying a large, multiengine aircraft, without adding pages of boring narration. As the early outline became the first draft, I realized that the copilot's internal motivation (trying to satisfy a perfectionist father) could become another story line and source of conflict among the "pilgrims," adding to the pace and complexity of the trip. This decision turned out to be crucial to the Epilogue/ ending of the book.

I wrote the book with a future movie script in mind, so I did everything I could to make readers feel they are "watching" the story unfold. In my mind, I see very clearly the windows of the bus as it pulls past an accident on the road. Behind every window is a wounded veteran looking out at the burning car. Reflected in every window is what the veteran is thinking about—the burning wreck of a truck, tank, or helicopter where a friend died in the war. I intended this to be one of the most visually compelling scenes in the book—an emotional demonstration of why people are broken by war.

The character of Santa, the story of the navigator's escape from Saigon as a child, and the arrival of the bus at HOOTERS have something in common. All are intended as surprises for the readers—little rewards scattered along the pilgrims' trail to home. Without these unexpected little twists, the book could turn into a maudlin catalogue of sad stories. Shakespeare taught me the value of comic relief and subordinate characters with a life of their own. I tried to use these lessons in the book.

I think the scene of the pilot's wife struggling with children, groceries, and a dead car battery in a cold, rainy parking lot is absolutely essential to the development of the book. It transforms her from the whiner some readers believe her to be after Chapter 1, into a heroine struggling to keep her family normal and intact despite the pressures of single parenthood during deployments and war. Like Santa, and the nurse, and the Ranger, she shows a determination and strength of character that shines like a tiny ray of hope through a very gloomy chapter in the book, and in the lives of the characters. "I can fix anything," she says (page 126). Readers are left with the impression that she can.

Finally, the readers' opinion of the pilot takes a turn at the end of this chapter. Until now, he has been the perfect professional, calm and strong in the face of pressure. His refusal to answer his wife's texts, and his determination to interpret her motivations in the worse possible light, cast doubt on his mental state. Apparently something in his life is broken, too . . . as readers will discover 142 pages later.

CHAPTER 5: FIXED

① WHAT HAPPENED?

Time and place matter: 1320 hours 23 December: El Paso, Texas

Alone among the chapters in this book, Chapter 5 takes place at a single location. There is no flight, no change of setting, no pressure to get the story moving—just interaction by characters. As a result of that interaction, those wounded by war go from "Broken" (Chapter 4) to "Fixed" (Chapter 5) . . . at least for the time being.

The first of these interactions involves the reporter and three amputees. After observing with her reporter's eye their boyish response to a beautiful waitress, she moves to a second interaction at the "adult's table" with the Ranger, chaplain, owner, nurse, and doctor.

Picking up on their discussion about what is happening all over the room between young wounded soldiers and the attractive waitresses, she prompts a frank discussion of the need by those soldiers, male and female, to be reassured of their attractiveness to the opposite sex. Pressing the more mature characters at her new table for professional opinions, the reporter gains unexpectedly personal insights into the emotionally scaring experience of returning from war. The doctor in particular talks about the importance of his wife's support after he was wounded in Vietnam.

A further question about romance between patients and medical staff prompts flashbacks by the nurse to a relationship she previously had with a doctor. At this moment, the insightful comments by the Ranger about the emotional interaction between wounded and their nurses causes her to see him in a new, and more positive light.

Around the room, formerly stressed soldiers are relaxed and enthusiastic in the presence of so many attractive women. An unexpected invitation from the doctor to dance prompts the nurse to have another flashback to a dance in the war zone with her doctor fiancé. At HOOTERS, the older doctor is a bit stiff in his movements, but his dancing with the nurse at an energetic pace is appreciated by the entire audience, especially when the couple is joined by a burned soldier and a waitress. At the end, the doctor pulls up his flight suit to show several amputees in wheelchairs that he was dancing on artificial legs, the result of his wounds from Vietnam.

Meanwhile, the sullen soldier, who is faking his leg wound, makes multiple attempts at molesting waitresses. The first attempt prompts a loud rebuke from the Ranger. The second causes the Ranger to follow him into the men's room where the miscreant gets the worst of a physical altercation.

Taken together, the many events, conversations, and human interactions of the lunch at HOOTERS improve the mood of everyone on the trip. As the title of the chapter suggests, the travelers return to the repaired aircraft with their problems (or at least their attitude) "fixed."

HOW DID IT HAPPEN?

This is an intensely personal chapter with no hint of the high-tech adventure that pushed the story forward in previous chapters. The power of the chapter comes from four main literary tools.

The first is the highly descriptive imagery. The uniforms and bodies of the HOOTERS waitresses receive the same detailed description as the flying and medical scenes in the earlier (and later) parts of the book. The language is suggestive, highlighting the waitresses' form-fitting tops, the curves of their buttocks, their long hair that "just kissed the top of the breast," their dazzling white teeth, and their strategically placed apron with brightly colored pens that "drew the eye to the crotch." Their actions were calculated to be inviting, as they leaned forward toward the men, and engaged them with lingering looks while taking orders. Even the description of their movements suggests a sexual fertility, as they "burst into the room like a squadron of honey bees" (page 118), and "buzzed between tables, pollinating their guests with smiles and French fries" (page129). Yet their actual appearance was more "suggestive than revealing," more invigorating than salacious. This was "the commercialization of the American Girl Next door," the reporter observes. "This wasn't *Pretty Woman* [a movie about a glamorous prostitute]. This was Princess Leia [from *Star Wars*, the object of romantic passion but not crass sexuality]" (page 120).

The same level of detail and imagery is applied to the dance toward the end of the chapter, where the technical description of music and footwork suggests the power and enthusiasm with which the dancers infuse the audience.

The second tool in the author's toolbox for this chapter is use of the "reporter's eye" (page 118) to capture the details of the waitress' appearance, and the soldiers' response. The reporter's clinical detachment gives the description a sense of logical objectivity that would seem strained and artificial if simply inserted by an omniscient author. Indeed, the whole discussion of the HOOTERS waitresses' wholesome sexuality has the ring of discovered truth when coming from the female reporter. The same comments might seem simply chauvinistic if coming directly from the male author.

Third, in contrast to the romanticized image projected by the HOOTERS waitresses, much of the important dialogue (and one of the flashbacks) in Chapter 5 leans heavily on the technique of literary realism toward life after suffering wounds. In discussing their personal experiences, the restaurant owner, the doctor, the chaplain, and the nurse all speak frankly of the self-doubt and fear of the future that wounded veterans feel—especially regarding their attractiveness to the opposite sex. When the discussion turns to relationships between nurses and those in their care, the nurse's flashback to participating in an amputation without morphine is jarring in its realism.

A fourth tool that helps engage and move the audience in this intensely personal chapter is the force of character demonstrated by some of the protagonists. (Remember, there is no "main character" in this pilgrimage.) The restaurant owner feels so deeply about the poor treatment of veterans returned from Vietnam that he has to pause in his introduction. The doctor explains that his years of study and sacrifice in medical school stem from his wife's encouragement to get past the barrier of his Vietnam wounds. The nurse takes a big risk with her career in allowing the wounded in her care to recover their sense of pride through interaction with the women in HOOTERS. Despite his unsteadiness on two new artificial legs, the Ranger shows his determination to help others by challenging those in wheel chairs to a race, and by physically intervening with a disreputable soldier who makes unwelcome advances to several waitresses.

Additionally, the constrained setting, with almost all of the action taking place in the single great room of a restaurant, stresses the intimacy of the subjects discussed and promotes an emotional attachment by the readers.

③ WHAT DIFFERENCE DOES IT MAKE?

This chapter ends and the next begins precisely at the middle of the book. Based on the development of the novel thus far, a reader might expect an author depending on so many other traditional literary techniques to lean on a traditional approach toward dramatic structure—and an examination of Chapters 5 and 6 suggests that this might be the case. Clearly this chapter offers multiple personal details that create a culmination of sorts in explaining the dilemmas facing the primary characters.

The detailed description of the attractive young women who hover around the wounded men, and the professional discussion of common personal fears by a reporter, doctor, nurse, chaplain, and veteran legitimize the sexual tensions (and fears) of the wounded warriors. The nervousness of the younger characters, and the personal yet detached analysis of the more experienced pros, makes the response of the sexually insecure soldiers seem normal, rather than nasty or demeaning toward the women. This increases audience empathy with the characters (to include those wounded emotionally but not physically) in a deep and personal way. It also reinforces the idea that there is value to talking about deep personal concerns with friends and loved ones—again, a major theme of the book.

Additionally, the conversation makes clear that emotional burdens that seem so unique and personal to those who suffer them are in fact common to others in similar circumstances. The wounded do not have to remain isolated and suffer in silence. Others feel the same way.

Indeed, if there is a single core theme in the book it is spoken by the Ranger shortly thereafter, when he observes, " . . . everybody who went to war was shot . . . Some were shot in the body. Some were shot in the head . . . And some were shot in the heart. Everybody got shot. And everybody needs to recover" (page 128). As the narrative makes clear, this applies to the flight crew and the medical team, as well as the wounded. They all have been "shot" and need to recover—by interaction with others.

Those looking for overall structure might find this the climactic passage of the book. As a result, readers leave this chapter with a better understanding of the sacrifices endured by those who went to war, the personal challenges that still lie ahead for them, and a concern for and attachment to those headed home and into such long-term peril.

Yet the dance and the positive energy that flows from this chapter suggests a tone of hope amidst the jarring realism. Having paused for serious reflection, the author gets the story moving again with the animation of his dancers. The doctor's display of his prosthetic legs at the end delights the readers as much as the soldiers racing in wheelchairs. Here, among so many broken lives, shines a ray of hope.

The Ranger's show of character (and strength) in the physical altercation with the abusive soldier performs a similar function, lightening the mood, restoring order, and showing that honor and dignity can return to a wounded life.

By the end of the chapter it is not just the aircraft that has been "fixed" (the chapter title), but the attitude of the pilgrims. "The sad little parade" of the last chapter becomes a "trail of wounded soldiers, medical team members, and aircraft crew . . . animated and happy" as they head back to the bus to continue their pilgrimage home.

AUTHOR'S NOTES

In terms of dramatic structure, I conceived of this chapter as a clarifying point for readers in the middle of the journey through the text. At this point readers have met the major characters, grasped the basic tapestry of the narrative, been propelled forward by the technical description of medical care and flying, and experienced the emotional tug of the perils and challenges the characters face. It is time to clarify and drive home the fundamental message of the book. I do that by showing the internal isolation and concerns of all the wounded, having the "resident experts" (the doctor, the nurse, etc.) at the "adult table" explain this reality, and then demonstrating how the pain—physical or mental—can be eased by human interaction.

Notice the importance of the reporter. She is the professional (and thus trusted) eyes and ears of the readers. She describes the HOOTERS' waitresses and their effect on the wounded. She generates and directs the conversation that allows the "experts" to lay out one of the key points of the book.

The bad soldier (who fakes his wounds and misbehaves with the waitresses) was included because . . . well . . . there are bad soldiers. Not a lot of them, but like the coward introduced in a future chapter, they are resident in the ranks of every Army. I know that many critics of the war will approach *CENTERLINE* assuming that it is a shallow celebration of all things military. I wanted the book to be accepted as an accurate picture of military personnel and their families, their trials, and their triumphs. Accuracy demands portrayal of the bad side of the military as well as the good.

The inclusion of the dance scene was a direct result of my study of Shakespeare under Dr. Barbara Mowat in the English Department at Auburn University. There I learned how the master writer of the English language sometimes used the dance in his plays to suggest the establishment of social order. The dance is where Romeo and Juliet meet, where Benedick and Beatrice, and Claudio and Hero all celebrate their marriages in *Much Ado About Nothing*. Similarly, my intention was for the dance to draw to together those who went to war (flight crew, medical team, and wounded soldiers), those they served (waitresses and other patrons in the restaurant), and the readers in a celebration of life. For this brief moment the wounded are healed, the emotionally scarred are made whole, and social order is restored. It does not last, of course, but it provides hope and a glimpse of a happier future. The pilgrimage may turn out well, despite the pilgrims' misgivings.

Setting this scene in HOOTERS, by the way, was the

result of long hard thought about how to capture the real concerns wounded have about being accepted by the opposite sex—as well as a happy accident. As I returned from an interview with military nurses at Ft. Sam Houston in San Antonio, talking about this very subject, I passed a HOOTERS and decided to investigate it as a potential setting for this discussion among characters. I frankly expected something much more "tacky and unrefined." Instead I recorded most of the description of what I might call "wholesome teasing" that appears in the first five pages of Chapter 5. I visited several more times for additional research . . . always with my wife.

Last, an avid movie fan might note a certain resemblance between the doctor and Lieutenant Dan from the movie *Forest Gump*. My character is a different person, named for two of my grandchildren. But I confess to having wondered whatever happened to Lieutenant Dan, played with such energy and pathos by Gary Sinise. I like to think that he might have turned out like *CENTERLINE*'s Dr. Dan Woody forty years later.

CHAPTER 6: QUICK TURN

🌕 WHAT HAPPENED?

Time and place matter: 1440 hours 23 December: El Paso, Texas, to Garden City, Kansas

After the aircraft is briskly loaded, and promptly and professionally departs, conversations among passengers begin, and the focus shifts rapidly from character to character, propelling the story along.

The discussions begin as the nurse and chaplain watch a happy group of wounded soldiers board, their morale visibly improved by the experience at HOOTERS. The chaplain compliments the nurse on her new administrative flexibility, and she recognizes that her patients seek more control over their lives.

Next, the flight engineer makes a crude comparison between large round hamburgers he brought back from HOOTERS, and the breasts of the flight engineer's wife. A joking but cutting response prompts the not-always-mature and several-times-divorced navigator to comment on the tension between the pilot and his wife. He observes that in his experience, a wife's anger indicates she still cares enough to change her husband; unexpected sweetness in the relationship indicates an impending divorce.

The reporter returns to her efforts to get a story from those who have been to war, trying to gain moving insights from the chaplain. What she gets instead surprises everyone. Through flashbacks, readers gain insights into the emotionally challenging nature of the chaplain's work. Through these discussions, readers and characters sitting near the exchange discover that the chaplain has given up on his religious career because he perceives his service in war to have been a failure.

The narrative switches quickly to a discussion between the Ranger and the nurse, disclosing that they have much in common in their experiences and attitudes toward life. Their mutual admiration for each other's leadership and self-sacrifice wipes away past rivalries, as they find the basis for a serious friendship. In particular they both value commitment—to their jobs, to the people they serve, and to the people they love.

In the only story in the book *not* told as a flashback, the reporter finally gets a combat tale she can use, from a soldier credited with single handedly attacking and killing multiple enemy troops.

As the flight becomes routine, the crew turns to telling jokes over the headset. The doctor weighs on with a joke that all enjoy, but their merriment is cut short when they realize he is suffering a heart attack. Perhaps based on his experience in Iraq, the chaplain recognizes the problem and springs into action, even before the medical personnel. Their response is timely and professional—and technically perfect—the result of relentless training by Nurse Ames.

The crew in the cockpit shows a similar technical perfection, declaring an emergency, identifying the best place to land to obtain cardiac care for the doctor, and working quickly and efficiently through the landing procedures. The pilot's actions are professionally perfect (page 158).

The plane lands and the doctor exchanges a quick and emotional message with the chaplain urging him to continue in his chosen profession, before being off loaded and rushed to a waiting ambulance. Again the technical proficiency of all concerned is stressed as the civilian medical technician, a former Navy corpsman, backs the ambulance to the aircraft and transfers the patient without waiting for the aircraft to shut down the engines. This speedy landing, off load, and return to flight is called a "quick turn" in military parlance.

As the doctor departs in the ambulance, several characters think about how quickly this event has changed lives, and how quickly their own lives were turned upside down by events in the theater of war. The Ranger has a flashback that explains the loss of his legs, and the debt he feels he owes to other wounded to help them improve their lives. The nurse has a similar flashback to the moment when her doctor fiancé was killed, and her life made a quick turn for the worse.

❷ HOW DID IT HAPPEN?

This chapter is the beginning of the second half of *CENTERLINE*. As pointed out early in this guide, Freytag's Pyramid for dramatic structure was designed for analyzing traditional tragic plays, rather than novels. But it offers a handy departure point for understanding the schematic structure of this novel. In the Prologue and first four chapters readers see not so much rising action as a knitting together of the stories of numerous travelers into a single narrative. In Chapter 5, that narrative reaches a clarifying moment, when the Ranger notes that everyone who has been to war has been wounded and needs to heal. Readers

discover that the characters cannot heal on their own—
they need interaction with other humans to further that
healing process.

In this chapter, as the aircraft moves the pilgrims
toward Garden City, conversation and character interaction
describe not so much the beginning of "falling action" (as
in Act IV of *Macbeth* and *Richard II*), as a sense of "accelerating action," quite different from the plateau of Chapter
5. The story leaps forward by jumping from character to
character. In each short exchange readers learn something
about a character that expands his or her depth, contributes
to their motivation, or increases a sense of mystery to be
uncovered in the future. For example:

> » The chaplain sees his "whole job differently
> now"—after his service in war that flashbacks will
> describe (page 141).
>
> » "No more Nurse Ratched" the Ranger tells the
> nurse, marking the end of their rivalry and the
> beginning of a friendship built on mutual pro-
> fessional respect. The similarity of their focus on
> service to others as compensation for some untold
> part of their stories is striking (page 145).
>
> » The writer-soldier's prosthetic hook "opened and
> closed reflexively as he tried to clench his [miss-
> ing] fist." Something about the self-aggrandizing
> story the corporal tells the reporter suggests that
> the other soldier knows more than he is admitting
> (page 151).

Clearly the storyline is gaining momentum, until interrupted by the doctor's heart attack.

The emergency snaps the readers and the characters back into a word of action-adventure, as the medical and flight crews race against time in applying a series of technical procedures to save the doctor's life. The successful results affirm the leadership of the pilot and nurse, and the training that has honed their respective teams to a sharp professional edge. It is not just ironic that the most professional responses come from the pilot, nurse, and chaplain, who appear to be the most conflicted characters. See Question 3 below for what this implies about these individuals.

Finally, true to form for this novel, the name of the chapter ("Quick Turn") has multiple meanings, which deepen and enrich the story line.

» The actual diversion of the flight, off load of the doctor, and return to the mission is a "quick turn" in military terms.

» In keeping with the realities of military life, a routine mission makes a quick turn into a matter of life and death.

» The Ranger contemplates (in flashback) the quick turn of fate that left him legless and owing his life to a medic who died saving him.

» The nurse reflects (by flashback) on the quick turn her life made when her fiancé was killed by a rocket in Baghdad.

» The doctor's life has made a quick turn from telling a joke to fighting for survival, thereby providing an important lesson for characters and readers alike.

❸ WHAT DIFFERENCE DOES IT MAKE?

At the dead center of the novel, Chapters 5 and 6 represent a major turning point in the narrative. In the opening chapters, readers encountered examples of technical expertise, stories of wounded bravely fighting against their new limitations, and internal pressures not evident to external view. In these two crystallizing chapters, the individual narratives come together around several central ideas.

» Everyone who went to war was wounded in some way—physically, mentally, or emotionally.

» Each character has an inside story he or she is struggling to manage.

» Several characters are using public competence to sublimate private stress.

» Losing one's self in work and technical details has its limits. What the veterans really need is human contact, reinforcement, and reassurance.

Characters who think they are rushing home for Christmas are really rushing toward a reckoning with these realities. They do not recognize the danger. The readers do. The result is a rising (or accelerating) sense of peril that draws readers in and along for the ride. Readers actually want to read faster, to use the clues discovered to unlock the mysteries that mark each individual's flight path back to the centerline—back to home. For example:

» When the chaplain compliments the nurse on bending the rules, and points out that all the wounded want is "some control over their lives" (page 139), readers should begin to suspect this may apply to the hyperprofessional nurse as well.

» The navigator's jesting but cynical observation that wives become more affectionate when they are covering plans for a divorce creates significant dramatic tension for the pilot later in Chapter 11.

» The nurse's flashback to misgivings that something "just didn't feel right" about the relationship with her fiancé plants a seed of doubt that puts her professional perfectionism in a new light.

» The final words of the nearly unconscious doctor to the discouraged chaplain—"You have a gift. Don't waste it."—increase the pressure on a religious leader about to give up on the animating force of his life.

These individual story lines, and others to be further unraveled in future chapters, shift the story from one about people with physical wounds headed to the safety of home, to one about veterans with internal emotional wounds, still in danger and beyond the reach of military or medical assistance.

AUTHOR'S NOTES

In conceiving and writing this chapter, I was consciously thinking of "Snowden's secret" from Joseph Heller's *Catch 22*. For those unfamiliar with this dark comedy, Snowden is a fictional crew member wounded on a U.S. bombing mission in Italy in World War II. Crew members try to save him by treating a wound in his leg, while he is bleeding to death from an undiscovered wound in his belly. Having properly bandaged the evident physical damage, those providing medical care missed a deeper problem. In the last chapter we discovered that all those who went to war were wounded. In this chapter we learn that those wounds may be deeper than medical care alone can cure.

(Those who know Heller's novel will remember a second, even darker secret—that absent the animating spark of life, Snowden will "rot like garbage." In contrast, *CENTERLINE* carries a much more uplifting message about the triumph of the human spirit.)

Given the fixed number of pages in a standard novel, an author is pressed to choose between action, character development, and the number of characters. This is a action-adventure book, with many characters in play. The danger is that space for character development will be sacrificed, leaving the characters flat and impersonal. I wanted characters that readers would identify with in order to increase the emotional power when they were placed in peril.

One answer was the flashback. You can learn much about a person by seeing them respond to a crisis. The flashbacks plunge the characters (and the readers) into a series of short crises. In each case, we learn a lot about the character in just a few words.

Humor served the same function in this chapter. The jokes people tell, and how others respond, reveals much about them in short order. In this chapter we learn through humor that the navigator is a bit of a ribald rascal, the flight engineer is not a man to be trifled with, the copilot is more of a risk taker than we might have imagined, the doctor is confident enough to make a joke at his own expense, the formal nurse is quickly disarmed by honest and gentle jesting, and the Ranger can actually lead with humor, using a soft joke to open a path to dialog. After the humorous exchanges in this chapter, readers likes these characters. So the physical and emotional peril they experience in future chapters is emotionally enhanced.

Also note the short lesson the pilot gives the copilot in dealing with emergencies on page 159. This is not an "ass chewing" on the order of previous lessons, but an encouraging discussion of her growing expertise. After reassuring her that she will one day be a command pilot as well, he provides a tip about talking on the radio in an emergency; "Take two deep breaths. Drop your voice an octave. Then key the mike."

This is the very first lesson in leadership I learned in the Army. The summer before I became a high school senior, I attended a two-week Junior ROTC camp at Ft. Polk, Louisiana. It was 1966 and soldiers one year my senior were flooding through training at Ft. Polk, headed for Vietnam. There were 120 of us high school cadets, organized into three rifle platoons, maneuvering across the marshland of Louisiana, opposed by regular soldiers playing an elusive enemy. I was platoon leader for the day, and when the lead platoon encountered an ambush, we were called quickly to reinforce them. The 17-year-old on the other end of the radio was greatly alarmed at being pinned down by the mock ambush, and I tried to push my team forward by excited radio transmissions. Later an experienced sergeant gave me the advice I wrote into the mouth of the "veteran pilot." When the guy on the other end is in trouble, the last thing he wants to hear is a high-pitched and panicky call from you. Calm down, take two deep breaths, drop your voice an octave, then key the radio and take charge of the situation.

It is a lesson I have never forgotten. It is a lesson the copilot will remember on the last page of the book.

CHAPTER 7: EVASIVE MANEUVERS

① WHAT HAPPENED?

Time and place matter: 1620 hours 23 December: Lubbock, Texas to Garden City, Kansas

Advised that the passengers were depressed by the doctor's heart attack, and seeking opportunities to train the copilot for future combat missions, the pilot plans for the type of takeoff used in combat zones. (Remember that the book is set in 2007 at the height of active combat in Iraq. The copilot would be using this training during her upcoming first deployment.)

After checking with the nurse to ensure that the passengers could handle the maneuvers, the pilot explains the training exercise over the intercom. Simulating a takeoff in a hostile environment, he will run the engines up to full throttle, take off as quickly as possible, conduct evasive maneuvers against simulated missiles and rockets over the end of the runway, then circle the airfield at high speed and low altitude, before climbing at maximum rate directly over the runway. For a large four-engine aircraft like a C-130, it is an aggressive series of maneuvers that will pull the passengers violently upwards, sideways, and down.

Once the aircraft is airborne and the training scenario begins, the pilot flashes back to similar attacks he experienced in Iraq—to include a defense by American helicopters that killed the attackers. As the flashbacks show, during that early experience the pilot was not the hypercompetent professional we see now. He is determined to make sure the copilot is ready for situations in which he felt unprepared.

In the back of the aircraft, most of the soldiers are

excited by the high-speed rise and fall of the aircraft. Some raise their arms as if on a roller coaster. The reporter, on the other hand, is more than a little alarmed, and asks her seat mate, the writer-soldier, about the soldiers' enthusiastic response. He tries to explain the sense of purpose, action, and worth that he felt as a soldier with an important job to do. He explains how being wounded robs people of that sense of control and self-worth. Being on board a military aircraft taking evasive action, even for training, brings back that feeling of being alive and walking on the edge of danger—a sense most of the wounded will lose forever as they return home, and settle into routine lives bounded by whatever activities their wounds will allow.

Training exercise over, the aircraft sets course for Garden City, Kansas, to drop the remaining passengers. The reporter takes the opportunity to try to squeeze a story out of the writer-soldier. What follows is a verbal fencing match, where two former literature students and film buffs argue in a good-natured way over ideas and values using references to various well-known works of Western literature. The points they make are less important than the way they enjoy the intellectual sparring, and they come to realize (like the nurse and the Ranger in Chapter 6) that they have more in common than they first thought. In fact, they actually enjoy each other's company. This is especially true as the writer-soldier shares his passion for writing and literature, and the reporter shares her interest in films.

Something in the writer-soldier's manner suggests to the reporter that he has not told her everything about his background and experiences at war. He refuses an interview and does not want to talk about his wounds, which he attributes to a mundane traffic accident. Readers see a flashback to his youthful writing success ignored by a father more interested in an older brother's prowess on the football field. At the end of the chapter, the writer-soldier resorts to some obscure passages from Rudyard Kipling to suggest that reality is more inspiring than stories.

The reporter, "hooked" (as she said in Chapter 4) on the young man with the hook for a hand, vows to discover the reality he is hiding.

② HOW DID IT HAPPEN?

This short chapter is built around only two events: a C-130 takeoff using combat tactics, and a friendly (but wary) verbal dual between the reporter (still seeking a story) and the writer-soldier with a hook for a hand who sat with her at lunch. These brief actions, exchanges and flashbacks increase our understanding of the pilot and the writer-soldier, but deepen the mystery surrounding both, while continuing to accelerate the wounded "pilgrims" toward an increasingly uneasy homecoming.

The key to making both segments of this chapter work—the part demonstrating the proficiency of the pilot, and the part establishing the special relationship between the reporter and the writer-soldier—is detail. It is the depth of detail that makes the characters convincing to other characters, and by extension, to readers.

For the pilot's story, the depth of detail is connected to the physics, danger, and difficulty of performing evasive actions in a large aircraft. The operation of the flares; the timing of turns; the rapid balancing of speed, lift, and altitude; the exceptional handling of the flight controls at high speed and low level—all of these actions and more are described in a detail that makes readers feel like they are actually present, watching every move of the pilot, every response of the aircraft, every reaction of the crew and passengers.

The Prologue of *CENTERLINE* shows the pilot at his technical best—a supremely confident and competent command pilot, flying a dangerous and demanding mission. The chapters that follow establish the technical complexity of the job he occupies and to which the copilot aspires. The difficulty of maintaining high standards is emphasized by his detailed critiques of the copilot's performance. In this chapter readers learn that the pilot has reason for his perfectionist approach—less than perfection spelled near-disaster in his past. "I wish someone had practiced this with me before my first trip," he says on page 165. Readers begin to suspect that this might be the reason for his harsh attitude toward the copilot. He wants to spare her some trauma that he suffered.

In the combat flashback, the heart-stopping approach of the rockets, the coolly coordinated response of attack helicopters, and the devastating effect on the enemy missile and rocket teams make readers witness to a terrible drama with life and death at stake on both sides. By the end of the section, readers are convinced of the pilot's almost superhuman precision and coolness under fire. Yet his own comments suggest that he did not always have this zero tolerance for error. Something turned him into a pathological perfectionist. Clever readers wonder what.

For the writer-soldier—the young mechanic turned philosopher—the convincing detail is in the authors, titles, and literary ideas that roll off his tongue, and off the tongue of his antagonist, the reporter trying to use the story of his wounds for her own purposes. If one character had gone into this level of literary detail alone, the remarks would have seemed stilted and pretentious. The back and forth between the two, taking turns in correcting each other, makes readers party to an intimate little moment between two people surprised to find they like each other.

The early reference to the character Marion Hodgkiss, from Leon Uris' *Battle Cry,* introduces a sense of realism to the exchange. In that book, Hodgkiss dies an unexpected and too-young death as a Marine in combat on Guadalcanal. The reporter's comparison of that character to the writer-soldier introduces a connection to reality, without which this exchange might be mistaken for a passage from a romantic comedy. There is nothing comedic about what the writer-soldier and the others have been through, and immediately after the reporter's comment, he strikes directly at the heart of the reporter's style when he charges her with being more interested in spinning romantic tales than in the realistic facts. He trumps her observations with an obscure line suggesting that real stories are more interesting than those artfully designed tales. She knows the passage and even the author—Rudyard Kipling—suggesting that with such detailed knowledge of stories, she will get to the bottom of his story as well.

③ WHAT DIFFERENCE DOES IT MAKE?

Earlier in this guide we discussed the concept of graphing plot development, using Freytag's Pyramid as a model. This model does not apply directly to *CENTERLINE*—but graphing the action in similar form in order to understand how it develops provides some useful insights. To review:

> »   The introduction to the *CENTERLINE* plot provides a base. It starts with the Prologue and runs through Chapter 2. It sets the stage for readers by introducing the technical complexity of flying, the pilot's mastery of that complexity, the conflicts in his home life, the technical challenges of military medical care, and the idea of various characters making a pilgrimage to home. (The word *pilgrimage* is used to suggest more than a simple trip. This trip has spiritual connotations. The pilgrims will be changed by the pilgrimage.)
>
> »   In Chapters 3 and 4 the action rises in complexity and emotion, as the overall narrative is established based on the interaction of multiple character lines, and the emotional aspect of physical wounds is introduced.
>
> »   Chapter 5 acts as a lens, bringing into focus the ideas that everyone who goes to war is wounded in some way, and those so wounded need to heal in ways beyond the physical reach of medical care. All of the major characters pass through this lens in some way.
>
> »   Chapter 6 sees the action curve up and accelerate, based on mental and moral regrets from some of

the most solid leaders on the mission. These are described in flashbacks to events the readers see, but the characters (unwisely) hide. The pilgrims' interaction with the reporter emerges as a metaphor for their reaction to their experiences in war, as they refuse to share the truth of their situation, or create false narratives to cover reality.

» In Chapter 7, the action continues to rise and accelerate. The primary contribution of this chapter is to advance the inner conflicts in three major characters: the pilot, the writer-soldier with a hook for a hand, and the reporter . Clearly the pilot was not always a "hot stick" (Air Force term for great pilot), anticipating every crisis, and flying as one with the aircraft. The flashbacks show a younger, less experienced pilot struggling to keep up with the life and death challenges of flying in combat. Meanwhile the verbal "dogfight" between the writer-soldier and the reporter suggests that he is protecting an important part of his story that he does not want to share.

None of these internal conflicts are clear at this point in the narrative, but the astute reader can tell by the end of the chapter that there is something wrong with each character. There is something they are not admitting, even to themselves. As the aircraft and the plot race toward their destination, the dramatic tension within each character increases.

Again note the double (even quadruple) meaning of the title. As the pilot departs the emergency stop at Lubbock,

he conducts evasive maneuvers in order to train the copilot for combat. Internally, the pilot uses the maneuvers
to evade the inadequacy that he feels looking back at his
previous performance. Many of the wounded use the same
maneuvers to evade (for a while) thinking about their
arrival home and the life to come. The writer-soldier uses
words to conduct evasive maneuvers to avoid the reporter's
prying questions, keeping her at a distance from what he is
thinking and feeling inside.

AUTHOR'S NOTES

Many readers have asked how a career, non-pilot Army guy
produced a book with so much realistic detail about flying.
Answer: the same way I produced a book with so much
detail about military emergency medicine (see Chapter 9). I conducted hours and hours of research and taped
interviews.

My son Sam provided most of the detail about flying.
He has thousands of combat hours and flew all the missions I described for the pilot in this book.

The details of the exchange over literature between
the reporter and the writer-soldier came directly from the
many hours of drill I spent with Dr. Ward Allen, again
of the English Department in Auburn University, preparing for my oral defense as a graduate student thirty years
ago. For two semesters I read hundreds of pages each week,
then stood a weekly oral exam from Dr. Allen on what I
had read. It was a real challenge, and one of the most intellectually rewarding experiences of my life. Compared to
being grilled by Dr. Allen, writing this chapter was a snap.

Two other quick details:

» Note the pilot's comment to the copilot on page
  167, that all she can handle in low-level flight right
  now is an altitude of 200 feet. Compare this with
  the altitude of 100 feel that she handles as command pilot in the Epilogue (page 275.) This detail
  is not an accident. It suggests her transition from
  new student to experienced leader.

» Note that the pilot's phone buzzes with a message
  from his wife just before his "combat takeoff" and
  evasive maneuvers. He ignores the message (page
  165). This detail was one of many added in a late
  draft of the book in order to emphasize the growing gulf between the pilot and his wife. Do you
  think it accomplishes the intended purpose?

CHAPTER 8: COMFORT AND JOY

🔘 **WHAT HAPPENED?**

Time and place matter: 1700 hours 23 December: En Route Garden City, Kansas

Chapter 7 ends with the reporter determined to discover what the writer-soldier is hiding—an "undoctored incident that actually occurred," in the words of Rudyard Kipling's poem, "The Benefactors." Her expectations are met in the opening moments of Chapter 8, when the loud corporal who bragged about his exploits and his medal reveals that the actual hero of the event for which he was decorated was the writer-soldier. He surrenders his medal to the reporter, and at that moment the plane 'began to descend" (page 194). For better or worse, the homecoming is at hand.

The narrative line quickly switches to follow the nurse as she makes the rounds, checking her wards, while worrying about what lies ahead of them.

It switches again to an exchange where the Ranger tries to encourage the chaplain to continue his calling as a pastor and counselor. A flashback reveals what only the chaplain knows—that at the end of a long day he put off a soldier asking for time to talk. Perhaps failing one last time to find anyone to listen to his problem, the soldier committed suicide. As a counselor with no one to counsel him, the chaplain (like the nurse) has sublimated his feelings of remorse and guilt. Whereas she turned ultra-professional, the chaplain has convinced himself that he is no longer fit to counsel others.

The focus of the narrative jumps again, back to the

writer-soldier and the reporter. Resisting her pressure to let her tell his story, he claims that its release will benefit no one but her. Feeling her chance at a national byline slipping away, she lets her own story escape in an emotional torrent (page 200). It is a shocking moment for both the writer-soldier and the readers, as neither had previously pondered the reporter's motivation. When the writer-soldier responds with unexpected tenderness, the reporter leaps to her feet and departs, worried that she has made herself vulnerable in a way she had not intended.

As the aircraft nears the runway, the narrative jumps more rapidly from character to character, emphasizing the uneasy anticipation with which each individual awaits the end of the journey. As the ramp descends, a huge crowd of well-wishers is revealed, all singing "Joy to the World," and wishing "tidings of Comfort and Joy." The pilgrimage is over. The wounded warriors are home.

Some of the arrivals are triumphant. The burned soldier who danced at HOOTERS is met by an enthusiastic girlfriend, herself obviously a dancer. Those in wheelchairs and other wounded are met by family members with loving embrace.

Some of the arrivals (the sullen soldier who faked a wound, and the now-guilty soldier who lied to receive an award) are met by similarly shallow acquaintances.

While walking across the runway the writer-soldier has a moment of connection and chemistry with the reporter. Upon meeting his family, both of them are surprised by the mother's idea that the reporter write her story about the family's reaction to the writer-soldier's return. The plan solves the reporter's dilemma, and suggests a chance for the seeds of romance to grow. Left alone with the writer-soldier's dismissive father, the reporter begins to tell the story of his son's heroism—the story she cannot write.

The chaplain finds not only an encouraging wife waiting to welcome him home, but a much larger crowd than he had expected. It turns out that he had underestimated and undervalued his contribution to the community. As the doctor and the Ranger tried to tell him on the flight, other people seem to know him—and value him—better than he knows and values himself.

Finally, the end of the pilgrimage provides a resolution of sorts for both the Ranger and the nurse. He receives the bad news of betrayal from his fiancée's new love interest—a traveling salesman who does not carry the baggage of physical or emotional wounds. Upon seeing the exchange from a distance, the nurse flashes back to her own betrayal—the discovery while inventorying her dead fiancé's property that he was already married, and in fact was stringing along several nurses deployed to the combat zone. After struggling with her emotions, she approaches the Ranger and eventually invites him to join her for Christmas at her sister's farm home nearby.

As they make their way off in an unexpectedly positive resolution, the aircraft heads into the sky, its mission complete.

Or perhaps not.

② **HOW DID IT HAPPEN?**

The date and time put us on board the C-130 aircraft, in the dark, the day before Christmas Eve, within an hour of landing in Garden City, Kansas. We know from Chapter 2 that the remaining wounded will disembark at this location, as will the nurse. Readers should expect a final "set up" for major characters to complete their pilgrimages, and some sort of resolution upon their arrival. Thus character development and reader expectation are driving aspects of this chapter.

The plot of the novel is stitched together from the narratives of multiple characters among the wounded, the flight crew, the medical team, and family members waiting at home. The Christmas pilgrimage home for main characters from three of those four groups will end with the aircraft's landing. The emotional tension increases as these characters approach their destination.

The tension is released in a series of "reveals"—a moment when a question, problem, or situation is explained, frequently with some piece of previously hidden information. The author uses conversations and flashbacks to raise the emotional stakes for his characters, then uses reveals to resolve the situations. If readers were graphing the action, they would sketch a rising curve of action, followed by a plateau for those characters whose challenges are resolved.

For example, the anxiety of the wounded (and the anxiety of readers for them) is emphasized by the author's description of the final approach to home as "the part of the job that she [the nurse] hated the most" (page 194). The nurse can handle the "blood and gore," we are told, as well as the complex and prolonged medical care, from the emergency room through rehabilitation. But now comes the most dangerous time of all—reintegration into family and society.

They had been soldiers. They had carried weapons and worn body armor. They had a place, a role, a rank, a position. People took orders from them. People depended on them. What they did had significance. Their duties mattered, and so their lives mattered
Now all that was gone (page 194).

Once the no-longer-soldiers arrive home, they will be something else—something less. The professional nurse finds that she can do nothing but watch with rising frustration. "Some of them would return, regain their balance, and do well . . . Some would never regain their balance at all. And she couldn't help. She couldn't stop it. She couldn't even slow it [the airplane and the return] down" (page 195).

Again during landing, this sense of acceleration toward a dangerous unknown is repeated. "The plane was going slower and slower. The trip was going faster and faster. Almost there. Almost home. Almost out of control" (page 196).

This mood of anxiety is reinforced by the rapid shift of focus from character to character as they prepare for landing. Readers follow conversations by the reporter, the cowardly corporal, the nurse, the Ranger, the chaplain, then the reporter and the writer-soldier again, all in seven quick pages.

Flashbacks also crowd the chapter, providing "reveals" explaining the actions of four characters (the writer-soldier, the corporal, the chaplain, and the nurse).

And we see six reversals, where the fate of a character changes from negative to positive (or vice versa). The corporal is no longer treated as a hero. The chaplain who thought himself a failure is hailed as a success. The nurse whose life had been upended by the betrayal of a fiancé finds her prospects at happiness restored by the Ranger who has the same experience while we watch. The reporter's failure to gain a national level story is reversed by an invitation by the writer-soldier's mother. The soldier's reputation with his father is reversed by the story of heroism told by the reporter.

That's two major flashbacks, four reveals, and six reversals in twenty-four pages, making for a very active chapter, as readers arrive at the end of the pilgrimage and crash from closure to closure. The high-tech aspect of the book is missing in this chapter, as is the action-adventure (except for the drama of the writer-soldier's heroism in a flashback). Even the historical frame of the novel disappears. This is a classic romantic novel at this point, with readers emotionally engaged in the fates of the characters. Multiple narrative lines following the fates of multiple characters wind through the book to arrive together in this moment of homecoming. The effect is electric—the classic Greeks might have said "cathartic."

And finally, in the last line of the chapter, the big gray shape of the aircraft noses up into the starry night, suggesting that maybe the trip is not over for Air Evac 1492. In a graph of the action at this point, all of the characters are left on a plateau except for the crew and the pilot's family at home. For them, the curve of action begins to climb into the darkness with the aircraft.

3 WHAT DIFFERENCE DOES IT MAKE?

This is a complex and rapidly moving chapter, with multiple story lines terminating at a single location—the point where the wounded pilgrims, with their hopes, fears and stories, return to earth. The lessons readers learn from this unraveling are delivered in three ways: directly by the author's narration; directly by the words and actions of the characters; and indirectly, suggested but not directly stated by the author's narration.

In the case of the writer-soldier and the reporter, it is the interaction of the characters themselves (along with a new character—the writer-soldier's mother) that provides an important lesson. The stories of common people, especially those who suffer the wounds of war, do not need elaboration; they are inspiring by themselves.

The true story of the writer-soldier's undoctored incident is presented as a flashback. In this novel, people may lie in the present, but history tells the truth. The reason for his reluctance to tell his story of heroism is never quite clear. Perhaps he realizes that he has no proof except the word of a corporal who has already lied, and setting the record straight would require fighting the bureaucracy to change the official version. What we do know, is that many veterans show this same reluctance to talk about their war. They need special encouragement to embrace the healing that comes from sharing the truth with those they love.

The reporter's lesson emerges from both a reveal and a reversal, which take place at the same time. The reveal of course, is the emotional moment that she lays out her difficult past as the reason for her need to create inflated stories that will burnish her journalistic career. Suddenly she is not just a flat character, but a lonely and abandoned human being, trying to succeed on her own without a parent, friend or lover to lean on. The reversal comes with the writer-soldier's tender response:

> *All those times you were knocked down. Did you get back up? Did you regain your balance? Did you get on with life? Because that's a great story if you did. It's not just romantic. It's heroic (page 201).*

When next we see them, neither mentions the emotional reveal. But it has changed their relationship and reversed their destinies, welding them together in a way that the mother recognizes "the instant I saw you walking together" (page 205).

Concerning the chaplain, readers learn three lessons directly from his thoughts and conversations.

First, his experiences at war left him some very real reasons for frustration and regret. He saw terrible things that he could not change. And on at least one occasion, he failed a person he was sent to serve (the specialist who committed suicide after the chaplain put off his appointment).

Second, despite his belief to the contrary, the chaplain's net effect on the world and those he serves is far more positive than negative—he is much more a success than a failure. This is the message his wife and his hometown friends deliver, as they gather to welcome him home with "comfort and joy."

Third, as the Ranger suggests (page 199), the chaplain will be a better pastor, counselor and spiritual leader in the future, as a result of his frustrations and failures in the past.

He can and should focus with confidence on the promise of tomorrow, not the loss of yesterday. This is ultimately a healing and uplifting ending, which provides comfort and joy to the readers as well as to the character.

The final wedding of the narratives of the Ranger and the nurse offers a lesson in what really matters most in relationships. The delivery is a bit more subtle with these characters, however, coming as it does through the author's narrative, the characters' statements, and the readers' projections. For example, in speaking about his fiancée's betrayal, the Ranger finally says aloud what readers have been thinking all along: " . . . you know when it doesn't feel right. You may kid yourself, but you really know" (page 210). Of course, this is the same thing the nurse observed in thinking back to the doctor who betrayed her: " . . . something just didn't feel right" (page 149).

The reason "it didn't feel right" is that the Ranger and the nurse allowed themselves to be used by others who wanted something from them but did not share the deeper values and commitments that make lasting relationships work. The nurse drives this point home while inventorying her fiancé's belongings after his death. After counting his cheap watches, cheap pens, and rubber rings—and learning of the expensive watches, quality pens and "class act" wife he left at home—she thinks, "Guess he just used the cheap stuff out here" (page 209). She is, of course, including herself in this category.

By contrast, she is attracted to the Ranger for the way he thinks and acts, including his understanding of the role of nurses (page 128), his goal of helping wounded achieve full lives (page 135 and 195), and the respect he shows her in their conversation on the runway (page 211). In that last encounter he is both vocal and direct about the qualities he sees and admires in the nurse, and his willingness to subordinate physical attraction to deeper issues as they get to know each other.

What the text suggests without saying as they depart the scene of homecoming, is that this time "it does feel right," for both of them.

AUTHOR'S NOTES

This chapter was a real challenge to write. It requires resolving multiple character plot lines in a short space in ways that nonetheless seem realistic. My solution, as explained in (2) above, is the swirl of movement, anxiety, reveals, and reversals that propel the characters to their destination on the tarmac in Garden City. This requires a great deal of planning and "seed planting" earlier in the book.

Students of literature sometimes have a hard time believing that authors consciously use all the literary terms, tools, and techniques that their teachers suggest. I spent many hours reaching back to previous chapters trying to apply every trick of imagination, structure, and terminology that I could think of to set up the emotional "ah-ha!" moments that culminate in this chapter. If you think it is difficult to identify and trace these elements through literary analysis, you should try creating them from scratch. No, really . . . you should try.

Finally, note the selection of the destination: Garden City (suggesting the end of a quasi-religious pilgrimage home to a Garden of Eden), and Kansas (suggesting the essence of middle-America wholesomeness). How are these broken characters going to get back to the idyllic lives the name suggests? The answer is that they won't. Ultimately, their problems are not solved, their wounds are not "undone." As the doctor suggested back in the pivotal Chapter 5, "you never get over it. But you can get past it (page 124)." That is what makes this chapter and this book, cathartic and uplifting in the end.

By the way, Garden City, Kansas, is a real location, and a real mission that my son flew delivering wounded back to their homes. I thought about visiting it as part of my research for the book. I decided it was better to leave the nexus of all these stories to my imagination—and to that of the readers.

CHAPTER 9: "I'LL BE HOME FOR CHRISTMAS"

WHAT HAPPENED?

Time and place matter: 1120 hours 24 December: Scott AFB to Randolph AFB, San Antonio, Texas

It is just before noon on Christmas Eve.

The crew of Air Evac 1492 has returned to Scott Air Force Base to await additional missions or release to return home. The chapter opens with a call from the pilot's wife in which he reassures her that unless a mission emerges shortly, he will be back in time to spend Christmas with the family.

Unfortunately, he receives a call almost immediately assigning a new mission: carrying critically injured Marines to the burn unit at Ft. Sam Houston, in San Antonio, Texas. The plan is to fly the wounded to Randolph Air Force Base nearby, and transport them by ambulance to the Brooke Army Medical Center.

The pilot collects the crew and explains the necessity of their new mission and the fact that bad weather to the west might close in and prevent their return home to Little Rock for Christmas as planned. The next few pages are devoted to a technical description of the considerable medical challenges involved in transporting critically burned patients by air. With the aircraft jammed with patients, equipment, and medical teams, Air Evac 1492 departs the runway and turns toward San Antonio. There is no sharp dialogue between command pilot and copilot. Every minute counts in saving the lives of the wounded on board, and lessons can wait for later.

Seeking the fastest possible route, the pilot contacts air traffic control and asks for assistance in clearing commercial aircraft out of the flight path. Permission is granted, and multiple commercial airliners wish the aircraft and its cargo of wounded "Godspeed." In an FAA control center, a young controller asks his experienced supervisor whether he should intervene to challenge the "non-standard" salutes taking up space on the radio frequency. The supervisor flashes back to the memory of his own return from Vietnam as a young soldier, and the hostile reception he received. He instructs the controller to allow the radio calls to continue unhindered.

As the flight nears San Antonio, the pilot sends the copilot on a strange mission to "go back and check on the medical teams" (page 218). The scene the copilot discovers is "like something from a horror movie—except it was real" (page 219).

What follows is a detailed description, station by station, patient by patient, of the horrible aftermath of serious burns, as well as the heroic efforts of an exhausted medical team to save "their" patients. The copilot's tour of this tight little universe of pain and suffering begins with a victim muttering "I'll be home for Christmas." It ends with a nurse dressing a badly injured hand that smells like burned hot dogs. Overcome by sights and smells, the copilot vomits. The loadmaster, who suffered the same fate himself in the Prologue, assists her.

After the aircraft lands and the patients and medical teams depart, the pilot discovers the copilot crying in her seat. Horrified by the wounds and suffering she has witnessed, she has suddenly lost confidence in her ability to fly missions in combat, and even to serve in the Air Force. After a sharp rebuke, the pilot explains with compassion that learning to function in the face of such a horrible situation is essential if she is to serve and save those depending on her expertise. Speaking as a friend, he admits that he is also shocked and appalled by the realities of war, and that he sent her to see the burned Marines now, so she can function as required when she encounters such scenes in the combat theater. Finally, he expresses confidence in her abilities to do her job in the future.

Bolstered by his support, she turns to speak, but finds him once again immersed in the hyperprofessionalism that marks him as a command pilot. Nonetheless, she is greatly relieved at his expression of confidence and at his attitude as a fellow pilot and a colleague. She realizes that despite the short-term harassment common in the final training of a new pilot, she is going to find a home in a family of professionals doing something she values in the Air Force.

② HOW DID IT HAPPEN?

After twenty-five pages of reveals and reversals in Chapter 8, Chapter 9 begins with another surprise. Despite the narrative threads brought to an end in Garden City, the story of Air Evac 1492 is not over. Some authors call this technique a *false ending*. The idea is to slow the action and resolve some story threads to suggest that the main story is over. When the action resumes, the readers are reengaged with additional emotion brought about by surprise. (This technique is more common in movies than in books. See the various endings of the *Die Hard* movie series, starring Bruce Willis, for examples.)

The call from the pilot's wife reestablishes the importance of that narrative thread. Privy only to the pilot's side of the conversation, readers are drawn into the emotional exchange one sentence at a time. The young father has missed yet another milestone in his family's life—his children visiting Santa at the mall. Restoring the family unit seems to hang on his making it back home for Christmas. And it is already Christmas Eve. The reality of his situation is closing in.

Yet when the call comes from operations requiring another mission that might prevent him from making it home for Christmas, he seems to register no concern at all. It is hard to miss the point that something is off with this character.

What follows is a simple and direct description of mission planning, aircraft loading, departure. There is nothing here to suggest a high-tech, high-adventure, historical, or romantic novel. Yet this mundane description serves to set up one of the most emotional points in the book—the unexpected intervention of many pilots wishing the crew and their horribly wounded passengers "Godspeed" as they make way for the lifesaving flight to speed toward the burn unit in San Antonio.

Several things make this passage work. The first is the isolation of the wounded and caregivers—24,000 feet in the air, beyond the reach of any earthly assistance. The second is the location, crossing the heartland of the United States.

The third is the repetitious calls by multiple airlines, which suggests a connection to the nation as a whole. When British Air and Qantas call in, the broad connection to allies in Great Britain and Australia is just as immediate. Last, the selection of the approbation—"Godspeed"—imparts a religious tone to the exchange. The wounded are not just wished well—they are commended into God's hands.

Dispatching the copilot to see the medical team in action in the back of the aircraft has a dual purpose. Obviously it sets up the final scene in the chapter where the command pilot explains the realities of war and eases the way for the young copilot into the ranks of combat aviators.

It also provides an opportunity to explain in technical detail the intricacies of airborne medical treatment in general, and burn treatment in particular. Up until this point, the medical teams have been praised for their work, but the care actually described was mostly for those nearly recovered from their wounds. In this five-page passage, the medical challenge posed by critical burns is described in realistic detail, as is the high-tech treatment and personal dedication provided by the medical teams. The characters are not even named—neither the wounded nor the caregivers. Instead they act as symbols for all the wounded and all the medical teams involved in the war. Consequently, the tone of the novel shifts to become much darker in this chapter. The wounded are in such peril, and the flight crew and medical team work so hard to save them, that an emotional response is generated. The copilot is stunned by coming face-to-face with the physical carnage and human cost of war. And so are the readers.

③ WHAT DIFFERENCE DOES IT MAKE?

The main message of this chapter is direct and uncompli-
cated, spoken by the pilot to the copilot:

> *The blood and gore of war are terrible. Absolutely*
> *terrible . . .*
>
> *And you have to be able to function right in the mid-*
> *dle of it . . . To look at a guy with his lips burned away*
> *and nothing left but teeth, and realize that is a human*
> *being in there—and know it could have been you. And*
> *then do your job anyway. Because that is how we save*
> *them [page 225].*

It is a message of understanding and respect, not just
to the flight crews, but to the medical teams, the wounded,
their families, and everyone who serves. This is the moment
when civilian readers realize that there is a difference
between their lives and those of people in the military. The
difference is the reality of war that self-aware military people carry with them every day. Readers do not have to like
war to understand it and respect the people called to sacrifice in it.

A second message is the idea of kinship and community shared by people competent in their profession. This is
the sense of community the new copilot seeks. This is the
promise she finds at the end of this chapter, leaving her to
feel she has made it "home for Christmas."

AUTHOR'S NOTES

This is a short chapter—only fourteen pages. It was the
hardest in the book to research. It is probably the hardest to

read because it is both real and emotional. It was the easiest to write, because it is purely factual and flowed entirely from my research and interviews.

All the flying procedures, including the process of clearing a pathway in the sky to accommodate medical trauma flights, came directly from interviews with pilots who flew this sort of mission. An experienced air traffic controller suggested some changes in language, which I incorporated into the second edition.

I included the aging air traffic control supervisor and his flashback to returning from Vietnam as a young soldier, because so many veterans of that era have described similar experiences to me. I see that whole segment describing the good wishes toward the wounded soldiers by current pilots, and the disrespect the supervisor remembered from the past, as an extended metaphor for how differently Vietnam vets were treated when they returned with their wounds, both mental and physical.

The details concerning the physical reality of critical burns—how they look and smell, and how they are treated—came from interviews with people who have actually treated soldiers with such wounds. I don't know how they stand it, but I am thankful that they do.

In providing this in-depth description, I was faced with a writer's dilemma: What voice should I use for this long technical explanation? The copilot was looking at the treatment, but did not know enough to explain what she was seeing, either in conversation or in thought. The hyperprofessional nurse departed the aircraft in Chapter 8. Who else was on board who could describe the equipment and treatment in a way the readers would trust? Should I create a new character just for this chapter? Dare I change voices to an author's technical narration for this long segment? Would it distract the readers from the action?

I finally decided to run the risk of slipping into an author's narration of what the copilot was seeing while working her way around the victims, the medical team, and the aircraft. I thought the detail was so compelling that readers would not notice the change in voice. Not all of my fellow authors agree with this decision. But it works for me, and it seems to have worked for the readers who provided me feedback so far.

The major lesson from this chapter—that you must learn to operate in the face of war's ugliness if you hope to relieve its effects on the victims—was expressed by many of those I interviewed before writing the book, and many I have met since.

The major creative part I added to the chapter was the title. The pilot wants to be home for Christmas. So does a burned Marine. The one who makes it is the copilot, finally finding the home she seeks within the professional cama-raderie of the Air Force. Of course I listened to the song "I'll Be Home for Christmas" repeatedly while writing the chapter. I wanted to capture the poignancy of the trip.

Also note the false ending to Chapter 9. As with Chapter 8, the successful homecoming on page 226 ("She was home for Christmas.") suggests that the story is essentially over. That is not the case. This is simply another plateau, where one or more characters' problems are resolved, but the action for the aircraft and crew continues to curve up. This pattern of false endings is going to be important at the conclusion of Chapter 11.

And concerning the radio calls made by aircraft to Air Evac 1492: I know that Continental Airlines is no longer in business. The novel is set in 2007 when Continental was still active. I included it as a private salute to the airline and crews I enjoyed flying with as a passenger for many years.

CHAPTER 10: INTO THE DARKNESS

① WHAT HAPPENED?

Time and place matter: 1745 hours, 24 December: Randolph AFB to Home

After dark on Christmas Eve, while the crew is returning the aircraft to its normal inside configuration for routine missions, the navigator announces that there may be just enough time left for them to make it home to Little Rock that night. After hectic preparation and planning, the aircraft "pointed its nose to the northeast and climbed in a hurry . . . into the dark. And into the storm. And home for Christmas." In an important exchange with the flight engineer, the pilot explains that to save the Air Force money, he must carry less fuel than he wants, reducing his flexibility in case of an emergency.

For two pages the trip home progresses smoothly, and both the crew and the readers are awed by the beauty of flying. They are awakened from their reverie by a radio call advising of severe weather ahead. From that point on, several manageable problems accumulate into an almost unmanageable crisis.

> » The bad weather moves more quickly than expected, essentially racing the aircraft for Little Rock and home.
> » The crew must navigate around the intense storm, flying an indirect route, and consuming more fuel than anticipated.
> » A fire indicator light on Engine Number 1 blinks on and then off more than once.

» The gauges on the same engine begin to provide various questionable readings.

» The fire light comes on and stays on. The pilot responds professionally by working with the crew as a team and prioritizing problems.

» They deal with a potential engine fire first, shutting it down and flying on the remaining three engines.

» They conclude that they have a bleed air leak, which might pose a catastrophic threat to the aircraft, so they shut down the bleed air system and all the components it feeds—including the de-icer on the wings.

» They try to find alternative landing sites in case they cannot make it to Little Rock, or cannot land there.

» They continue to "zigzag" around especially bad parts of the storm.

These procedures reduce the short-term threat to the aircraft, but leave it flying lower, slower, further, and against more resistance than previously calculated. Increasingly, it looks as if the weather and fuel shortage may prevent a return to the centerline at Little Rock Air Force Base.

In parallel with the developing story, flashbacks reveal that the pilot previously faced a similar situation in a combat theater while carrying wounded aboard. Showing excellent flying skills and judgment in the current situation, the pilot is able to find the runway and land on it safely. Meanwhile flashbacks reveal less success in the previous parallel story. When a member of the ground crew in Little Rock shovels snow and ice off the runway to prepare the aircraft for a tow in Little Rock, he discovers that despite very adverse conditions, the pilot landed right on the centerline of the runway. In contrast, the flashback shows an especially rough landing during a sand storm in Iraq.

Also note that the copilot caught and corrected a pilot error in the landing procedures.

Three brief scenes provide important information before the end of the chapter.

» The wing safety officer arrives to congratulate the pilot on making all the right calls during the emergency.

» The copilot shows thanks and respect for what she has learned, but warns the pilot of becoming a perfectionist and losing his family in the process.

» The pilot has one last flashback to the consequences of his poor landing while attempting to recover to Balad air base in Baghdad. There his mistakes actually worsened the injuries of the wounded and hurt some previously uninjured caregivers in the aircraft. The pilot is deeply embarrassed by his failure. This explains his subsequent hyperprofessionalism, and his distant attitude toward others (including his wife). In the final pages of the chapter, he mistakes spilled red hydraulic fluid for the blood spilled during his previous poor landing, and the resulting red liquid on his boots stains the snow as he flees toward his truck in the parking lot, and then home.

② HOW DID IT HAPPEN?

This is one of the longer chapters in the book—32 pages—involving several locations, multiple flashbacks, and lots of technical action. What carries the chapter forward is the inexorable movement of the aircraft and the forces of nature around it. The pilot may wish he had time to stop and think (page 244). So may the readers. But there is no time. Gas is low and the weather is getting worse. It is a time for action, not pondering issues from the past. Only when the aircraft returns home can the past really catch up with the present, and affect the future.

Several aspects of the setting are extremely important to this chapter.

» It is Christmas Eve, and the crew is rushing to get home.

» It is winter, and a major storm is bearing down on the route home.

» The aircraft is carrying less fuel than the pilot wants, providing less flexibility in case of emergency.

» The aircraft is a C-130E—an older model without the more sophisticated radar and instruments available in newer aircraft.

» The readers know that there has been a maintenance problem with this aircraft in the past. A gauge has been replaced twice, and upon leaving Lubbock, the same "gauge for the Number 1 engine flicked twice into the red range, then returned to normal" (page 179).

Individually, these points of information are just details enriching the background tapestry of the story. But when the author carefully weaves them together so the difficulties spill over onto each other, the readers see a broader picture emerging than the crew initially imagines. The result is that readers experience a strong emotional response to the building dramatic irony. The readers watch helplessly as the crew navigates forward into peril.

The author's planned use of several literary techniques builds a tone of alarm and concern that marks the main action.

First is the two-page description, early in the chapter, of the beauty of flying at night. The extensive use of imagery creates a tone of peace and tranquility. The pilot looks down on the "glow, glimmer and twinkle" of man's activity as evidence of mankind's "imagination and creativity, of his drive and determination, of his initiative and hard work." He looks up at God's work, "a galactic cathedral," as the quicksilver of starlight fills the cockpit, and the sound of Christmas carols fills the headset (page 231). It is a moment of awe, humility, and pride. Lives have been saved. The sacrifice has been worthwhile. The mission has been a success.

At this moment of triumph, the action reverses and the graph of the characters begins to descend. Technical detail replaces imagery as the tone turns from romantic and emotional, to high-tech action-adventure.

The technical detail serves two functions. First, it gives the emerging crisis a sense of realism. Once readers understand why the crew cannot better anticipate bad weather in a C-130E model, or why an engine that won't "feather" makes the aircraft slower and takes more fuel, then the peril becomes more believable, and the threat to the crew more palpable.

Sometimes these details are carefully crafted, as when the author uses the movement of the junior loadmaster to the flight deck as an excuse for the more experienced navigator to explain the nature and danger of a bleed air leak. Sometimes the details are included in the dialogue, as when the navigator identifies the "green-green-white" lights of the military airport beacon. (This detail is pivotal in the pilot's confrontation with his wife in the next chapter.)

Additionally, the way the author "piles up" the details in rapid fire order creates a sense of overwhelming complexity. As details about bad weather, navigation difficulties, instrument malfunction, fire warning lights, closed airports, and fuel status pour in, readers quickly become as "task saturated" as the pilot (page 235). Instead of just watching the crew's dilemma as a detached observer, readers feel the sense of rising panic themselves. This is by author design, not by accident.

Another literary technique that makes this chapter work is the "parallel flashback." Although flashbacks have been important in previous parts of the book in explaining character experience and motivation, in this chapter, the flashbacks help the pilot (and the readers) relive a similar crisis from the past as the current crisis unfolds. Obviously the previous experience is weighing heavily on the pilot's mind as he nurses a crippled aircraft home through bad weather. Thus a triple mystery develops: What happened last time? What will happen this time? How does what happened last time influence and shape the pilot's life, now and in the future?

Although detail dominates the design and effect of this chapter, imagery and symbolism continue to play an important part.

As might be expected from the title ("Into the Darkness"), light and dark largely determine the mood of the chapter. As previously noted, the plane departs San Antonio and heads into the darkness and toward home. It rises into the starlight in the most tranquil moment of the chapter, and descends into the darkness of the storm once the mechanical problems emerge. Like the dust storm in the pilot's flashback, the snow is light in color, but so heavy that it is too dark for anyone to see outside of the aircraft. Even the weather radar tells "a confusing story," as does the pattern of lights on the ground when the crew finally drops out of the storm near the airport. Fortunately a beacon—"green-green-white" for a military airport—shows them the way home.

Interestingly, it is the glare of runway approach lights, reflecting from the dust and into the pilots' eyes—that poses the greatest danger in the flashback story. The pilot is prepared for this glare by his experience, and navigates the landing in the dark without incident. He is unprepared for the flashback brought on by the glare of lighting in the cargo bay after the crisis seems to be over. At precisely the moment that the danger is past, the memory of blood, pain, and the chaotic result of his poor landing with a load of wounded on board comes rushing back. Illuminated by the lights and his memory, the red hydraulic fluid on his hands and boots symbolizes the blood he thinks he has "on his hands." Blood red on the white snow, the symbols chase him toward the parking lot and his truck—"into the darkness and toward home" (page 259). Clearly, the darkness is as mental and spiritual as it is physical. As the chapter ends, readers wonder whether the pilot will find light and warmth, or cold and darkness at home.

③ **WHAT DIFFERENCE DOES IT MAKE?**

This chapter is about three things.

First, it addresses the dangerous, difficult, complex, and exciting technical challenge of flying. The action-adventure nature of the novel comes to a head in this chapter. Solutions to the multiple emergencies the crew faces are unclear. The pilot brings them home not just by superb flying, but by superb judgment. The author's relentless combination of detail and ambiguity drive this point home.

Second, the chapter highlights the importance of leadership in a crisis. From the pilot's example of encouraging the crew to help the loadmaster with his work (page 227–228), to his last minute teaching point to the copilot concerning the blinding flash of light over the end of the runway, the chapter is full of subtle demonstrations of personal leadership by the pilot. This is especially evident at the critical moment when the pilot settles the nerves of the entire crew by asking a casual question about tomorrow's Christmas dinner. As the navigator then observes:

> *His one question—off the checklist—conversational at a moment of maximum tension–steadied everyone . . . The pilot was walking a fine line, a line that technicians never understand but leaders get by instinct. And it worked (page 244).*

Third, readers see the price military people sometimes pay for doing their duty, even when the wounds are not visible. Both the author's timing and technique are critical to delivering this message with emotional power. The technique is the parallel flashback to a combat mission, as already discussed. The timing is the big reveal from the final flashback after the mission seems to be over. From the first pages of the Prologue, one of the recurring themes of the book has been the pilot's hyperprofessionalism—his idea that trying is not good enough—and his emotional distance from family and friends. Now in a single unexpected moment, we learn the origin of these personality traits. Stung by the pain he inflicted on others with a poor landing, he has adopted the standard of perfection as a way of life. Feeling guilty about this shortcoming, he takes on additional missions to compensate. Embarrassed by his failure, he has withdrawn from his family rather than share his burden. Only as he flees the aircraft and the flashback, do readers realize that he too has been wounded by the war.

At the end of the flight and the end of the chapter, the mission is over, and the aircraft is back home, parked on the centerline, awaiting repair and return to flight. The centerline has become a metaphor for return to safety and normalcy. Will the pilot make it home? Will he return to the centerline of his life as well? As he drives off into the darkness, these questions hang in the air.

AUTHOR'S NOTES

I hope readers will notice that at the moment of maximum beauty and tranquility in this chapter—at the highpoint of the pilot's accomplishment, as he views the stars above and the earth below, with the mission almost over and his spirit momentarily at rest—the pilot's greatest wish is to share the moment with his wife (page 232). Readers of early drafts told me that by this point in the book, they had begun to turn on the pilot because they interpreted his refusal to answer his wife's texts as meanness on his part. I added this brief thought in order to soften his character, and keep readers on his side, until the big reveal at the end of the chapter about his failure and guilt.

The copilot's closing comment and story comparing the pilot to her father was also a late addition to the book. I did not want her to depart the story with some simple, gushy, kiss-up comment to her boss. I wanted her to be a full, self-confident character, standing on her own two feet. That native confidence and competence—further developed by training—is important to the role she plays in the Epilogue.

Part of the dramatic tension in the chapter is created by the ambiguity of the situation. Did they have an engine fire or not? Was there a bleed air leak or not? Was the crew in mortal danger or not? The safety officer is introduced at the end to answer these questions. The pilot's judgment was sound. His flying was superb. He did save the aircraft and the crew. He is a day-to-day hero, even when not on the front lines. Establishing this fact at the end of the chapter is key to creating the emotional punch of his self-doubt in the next chapter.

By the way, the selection of the bleed air leak as the primary crisis imperiling the aircraft demonstrates the importance of research and consulting a technical expert.

I wanted a problem that was at once life-threatening and ambiguous—where the crew had to assume the worst, and make decisions that might compound the problem, but without full knowledge of the real problem they were facing. I wanted a situation that would require professional competence, but also steadiness and character. Through his encyclopedic knowledge of the aircraft, my Air Force pilot son (Sam) offered exactly right solution.

CHAPTER 11: CENTERLINE

① **WHAT HAPPENED?**

Time and place matter: 0100 hours 25 December: Little Rock Air Force Base (AFB)

After midnight—Christmas Day.

The opening of this final chapter in the book is an echo of the first chapter. The important differences will be discussed in Question 2 below.

Again, the chapter opens with the security routine required to enter a military base. It follows the pilot through his military housing area to his street, made almost unrecognizable by the storm. He pauses in a white-out, and reflects on his loneliness, and the need for someone to share his burden. It is late, and as the snow lifts for a moment, he guides on the only light on the street—a sad little Christmas tree with a single string of lights shining in the window of his otherwise dark house.

He enters the kitchen as before, this time bearing bags and a large, live Christmas tree. When his wife enters the kitchen and is warm and welcoming, he thinks back to remarks by the navigator (page 140), and fears she wants a divorce. As he follows her into the living room to set up the tree, he finds her both happy to have him home, and remorseful for the accusing tone of their last meeting. She explains that she has talked to the wife of another crew member, and now understands the responsibility he bears and the importance of his duties. She confides that she feared he had found some other place to spend Christmas (implying that it might be with someone else as well). He assures her that he loves her and is happy to be home.

With the new tree and lights set up, and presents rearranged, the husband and wife sit down to exchange their own gifts. Hers to him is an expensive specialty flashlight designed for use by pilots in the combat zone. His is a gold pendant in the shape of an airport beacon, with jewels to represent the lights of a military airfield.

The husband and wife settle in to enjoy each other's company. Summoning his courage, the husband asks if she really thinks he needs professional mental help. She answers with relief that her comments only meant that he needs to talk to her more about his life and experiences. This leads to a request that he break out of the self-imposed isolation that started with his last deployment and explain his burdens. Focused on the bad landing and the casualties he caused (highlighted in a flashback at the end of the last chapter), he still finds himself unable to articulate the burden of shame, guilt, and responsibility that he carries.

The wife urges him to "just try." As the storm rocks the house with its intensity, the pilot begins to share the story with his wife. The last lines of the chapter suggest that the worst of the storm is over, and conditions are about to improve.

2 HOW DID IT HAPPEN?

Because Chapter 11 is such a clear reflection of Chapter 1, comparison and contrast are important tools for both the author and the readers.

> » The arrival at the guarded gate to the housing area is the same in both chapters, but in Chapter 1

the snowflakes are "like lacy moths" (page 26); in Chapter 11, they are "ice bees" that pour in through an open car window, and strike the windshield with a sound like crystal (page 261).

» In Chapter 1 the guard post is dark and quiet (page 26); in Chapter 11, it is lit by harsh floodlights, dividing the scene into glaring white and pitch black (page 261). In Chapter 1 the guard is a model of professional security ("No bad guys getting past this gate, Captain." page 27). In Chapter 11, the guard slips and needs "something to hang on to" to maintain his balance (page 261). Note the pilot's answer: "I'll be OK . . . I'm headed home" (page 261).

» In Chapter 1, the drive through the housing area is easy and well lit. In Chapter 11, the familiar neighborhood is "strange and wild," with every familiar landmark obscured by the drifting snow. The name of the street the pilot lives on is nearly blotted out, the joyful lights lining his block are dark, and the storm has covered the dashed centerline of the street leading to his home. Chapter 1 ended with the warning that the storm "might get better and . . . might get worse" (page 36). The storms inside, outside, and between husband and wife, have all become worse. Having lost his way in all three of these storms, the pilot realizes that he has a personal "In Flight Emergency"—but without anyone to help him through the crisis. Blinded and cut off by the storms, he is physically and emotionally "all alone" (page 262).

Then comes a moment of contrast between the chapters—a turning point in the pilot's narrative. As the snow lifts for a moment, he is guided home through the storm by the only holiday lights on the block still lit—a dim little glow from the small Christmas tree in the front window of his own home.

Once inside, there's another contrast. The icy reception he received in Chapter 1 is replaced by "the warm glow" of a small kitchen light, and the warmth of his wife's greeting. His wife offered "no joy" in the first meeting. This time she is happy and inviting. This is a huge contrast; something has changed.

The "something" is a matter of trust. After talking several times to the flight engineer's wife, the pilot's wife concludes that she did not understand the importance of her husband's work, how much other people trusted him, and how her demands for more time and attention were driving them apart instead of together. In contrast to her comments in Chapter 1, she promises to trust him more. In contrast to the charge from the nurse in his crisis in Balad that "trying is not enough," the wife promises to be satisfied if he just continues to try to place more focus on the family.

The first test of that trust follows immediately, when the wife asks the husband to share the reason for his withdrawal and distant attitude since his last deployment. Again readers see the tool of dramatic irony at play, because they know the story from the flashback in Chapter 10, but the wife must wait for the husband's painful sharing of one detail at a time.

In the end, neither the wife nor the readers get to hear

the pilot's final description of the incident that has left him an emotional casualty of the war. Instead, the book closes with him in the middle of his story, transported to a crisis in the desert, memories of radio calls ringing in his ears, while his wife holds him tightly, and the icy snow beats against the house like sand. In a single image, the central dilemma of the book is captured. How does a warrior wounded in mind or body return through the storm of emotions to the balance point—the centerline—of his life? How can his family and friends help?

In an ending simultaneously frustrating and gratifying, readers are left to imagine what comes next in the life of this little family unit huddled against storms from inside and out. As the husband begins to speak again, the final image suggests a positive and uplifting end: "The storm was still fierce. But it looked like it was starting to break" (page 273).

WHAT DIFFERENCE DOES IT MAKE?

Because Chapter 11 so closely echoes Chapter 1, it would be valuable to review the observations offered in Question 3 of the first chapter review and analysis in this guide:

> *Many readers will not make this connection until the final two chapters, but this novel about wounded warriors coming home begins by showing the life of a wounded warrior (the pilot) at home. His wounds are invisible, but serious nonetheless. As readers will learn in Chapters 10 and 11, these wounds are the result of a mistake he made while flying a load of wounded to a*

hospital in Iraq. His mistakes as command pilot resulted in further injuries, and he carries that load of guilt on every mission, unable to talk to anyone about it. Seeking to atone for his mistake and return to the centerline of his life, he takes every mission available, and trains new pilots to a standard of perfection he did not attain until after he made his mistakes. No doubt he is being too hard on himself. Until he talks to someone (perhaps his wife) about the issue, no one can reassure him and help him get back home.

As the narrative progresses, returning through the storm to the centerline denotes both returning to the safety of the airport, and returning to a happy and balanced life. Ultimately, returning to the centerline becomes the goal of all the major characters in the book.

For the wife's part, see the subtitle of the book: "Not Every Hero Is at the Front." Her fight has been on the home front, trying to run the house, raise two children, and maintain a home for a husband who can't help and can't explain why.

The ways in which the two chapters compare demonstrate the roundness of the story, and the way the opening chapter sets the background and the direction for the entire book. The ways in which the chapters differ (in particular, the wife's attitude and the husband's response) demonstrate the distance the narrative has traveled in three days.

Not to be forgotten in the rush to the final lines is the pause where the husband and wife exchange Christmas gifts. It is this passage that supplies the uplifting and hopeful message of the book. Note that despite the tensions of a very long and unpleasant year, each has made a real sacrifice over time to provide a meaningful gift to the other. These are the actions of two people willing to work hard to stay together, not two loveless parties on the brink of a break.

The gifts themselves represent light as both a physical object, and as a metaphor. The wife gives the husband a light to use in the dark, to protect him in the confusion of battle. The husband gives the wife the physical image of a homing beacon, which then marks her as his home, and makes her a metaphor for the final destination of his own pilgrimage, both now and in the future.

AUTHOR'S NOTES

By using the term "roundness" above, I mean a return to the origin, with a sense of both completion and of change with growth. A quick summary of chapters shows how this works in this book:

- » In *CENTERLINE*, the readers meet the aircraft and crew in the Prologue, also titled "IFE" for In Flight Emergency.
- » The pilot and his wife, together with their stormy family relationship, are introduced in Chapter 1.
- » The "Lucky Few" on the medical team (as well as the reporter) join the story in Chapter 2.
- » The idea of hiding emotional wounds emerges as "Nothing to Report" in Chapter 3.

» Several wounded warriors who become central characters in Chapters 4 and 5 are "Broken" and "Fixed" (along with their aircraft) in those chapters.

» In Chapter 6, the readers see how a "Quick Turn" in life can produce a hidden wound.

» Chapter 7 shows how the wounded try to evade facing the full implications of their own stories.

» Narratives among the wounded, the medical team (that is, the nurse), and the reporter are resolved in Chapter 8, with those who find human companionship to weather their trials also finding the most "Comfort and Joy."

» Chapter 9 leverages a false ending from Chapter 8 into an emotional portrayal of the realities of wounds and war, with the copilot nonetheless finding her narrative resolved as she arrives "Home for Christmas" in the Air Force.

» From the copilot's cathartic experience and false ending in Chapter 9, the aircraft and its crew are plunged "Into the Darkness" of cascading threats in Chapter 10. Saved by teamwork, cool leadership, and professional skills, the crew returns safely to the centerline, only for the pilot to be plunged back "Into the Darkness" by a flashback to a mortifying mistake in his past.

» Following the false ending of Chapter 10, and a return to the location and challenges at the beginning of the book, the pilot and his wife find in Chapter 11 that the strength of their love has survived and grown stronger. Together they are now ready to face the challenge of the pilot's emotional wounds as he returns to the "centerline" and home.

Many literature students I have taught simply did not believe that authors of novels sometimes plan their work with the precision of an engineer. Well I did. And here is the proof.

EPILOGUE: EN ROUTE

● **WHAT HAPPENED?**

Time and place matter: 1600 hours 22 December 2011:
Somewhere else

Four years after the opening of Chapter 1, quite obviously in Afghanistan.

A radio call goes out across the Afghan desert request-
ing help to evacuate wounded in an emergency.

The pilot of an aircraft decides to take the mission and
rapidly assigns duties to members of the crew. The pilot
takes two deep breaths, then responds calmly and professionally to the radio call, informing the party in trouble
that assistance is "en route your location."

The command pilot is now-Captain JT Williams, the
inexperienced copilot from four years earlier. She handles
the aircraft deftly, and thunders across the desert at low
altitude headed to rescue the wounded soldiers.

● **HOW DID IT HAPPEN?**

These short two pages depend on three techniques for their
impact: technical detail, repetition, and surprise.

The technical details of radio procedure, crew assignments, and flight specifics return readers to the world of
the high-tech action-adventure novel. The decisions and
actions are quick and professional. The story moves as
quickly as the aircraft.

The repetition of these details reminds the readers of
both the professionally executed low-level mission in the

Prologue, and the critical, life-saving nature of the flights in Chapters 8 and 9. The language and the actions lead readers to expect Captain Mike Middleton, the pilot from earlier chapters, to be at the controls.

The surprise comes when the command pilot is revealed to be now-Captain JT Williams, who performs just as professionally as her mentor, Middleton, right down to the two breaths she draws to steady her voice before responding to the emergency call.

A second surprise comes from readers' delayed recognition that Chapter 11 provided another false ending. The story is not over at the end of Chapter 11, and in fact continues past the end of the Epilogue, and the book as well.

WHAT DIFFERENCE DOES IT MAKE?

Epilogues are generally added to plays, books, or speeches to summarize or comment in a way that brings closure to the whole. This epilogue does exactly the opposite. It expands the story and keeps it going past the end of the book and into the future. The war continues. The need for medical evacuation continues. The cycle of producing professional crew members and medical teams continues. The stream of wounded warriors, some shot in the body, some in the head, and some in the heart, continues as well.

The last two sentences of the Epilogue echo the last paragraph of the opening scene from the Prologue: "The right wing lifted high as if to wave . . . then [the aircraft] slid rapidly to the left, toward the next mission, and was gone (page 275).

With the previously junior pilot-in-training now the command pilot, the cycle continues.

AUTHOR'S NOTES

When my Army son read the completed first draft, he said, "Something is missing. You need to find a way to suggest that the cycle of wounding and healing continues. Maybe send Captain Middleton back out on another mission."

He was right. I needed a bigger ending than the last line of Chapter 11 offered. But I did not want to spoil the dramatic ambiguity of that ending. Did the pilot recover from his emotional wounds? Did the family unit stay intact? The language in the text points to "yes," but the overall message about wounds and recovery points to "maybe not." I did not want to compromise that message.

And so I turned to JT Williams, the inexperienced copilot of four years earlier, as the mission commander in the Epilogue. The cycle of duties continues. Will she in turn suffer wounds of her own? Only time—and perhaps a sequel—will tell.

ADDITIONAL IDEAS FOR
TEACHING CENTERLINE

This guide does *not* provide detailed questions that may simply be distributed to students, because students would just buy this booklet and regurgitate those answers, thus defeating the whole purpose of learning how to analyze literature for themselves. Instead, this section will help teachers to quickly and easily develop appropriate questions and assignments to promote learning.

APPROACHES BY LEVEL OF STUDY

It is important that assignments be designed with student ability in mind. Requirements should stretch students, but set them up for success, not failure. One way to achieve this goal is to use a taxonomy that keys assignments to student learning level. Here is a taxonomy I have used to design student requirements in more than four dozen courses over the last two decades.

» Advanced High School/Community College/BA/BS Level
  › Know and understand the material assigned.
  › Know and understand frameworks and professional terms that aid understanding.
  › Remember both the material and techniques provided for understanding.
  › Apply these ideas to the material assigned.
  › Develop a thesis/argument with support and conclusion to demonstrate the ability to know, understand, remember, and apply the assigned material.
  › Think Critically—Explore alternative explanations to initial conclusions.

» MS/MA Level
  › Know/understand/remember the readings and literary techniques.
  › Apply more sophisticated frameworks and research techniques.
  › Analyze assigned material plus other sources and data looking for a cause-effect relationship.
  › Evaluate answers developed by analysis. Select one to advance through coherent argument.
  › Think Critically—Consider alternative concepts of cause-effect in regards to how the literary techniques create and enhance the narrative. Are there alternative bases for analysis and evaluation?

» DBA/PhD Level
  › Synthesize all theories and data to create new approaches.
  › Think Critically—Create alternative ways to understand the text and its various messages.

There is nothing wrong with stepping across the boundary occasionally with requirements that move up or down this taxonomy. Introductory-level students can be tasked with evaluating or creating ideas. Advanced-level students are not beyond demonstrating a mastery of the basic facts of the text. But most assignments should be designed for the appropriate level. Here are some suggestions.

SIMPLE ASSIGNMENTS

BASIC KNOWLEDGE FOR ALL LEVELS

This chart will help develop basic matching and content checks. Scramble the names, functions, and descriptive details, and require students to match them. Here is the information in the proper order:

CHARACTER	FUNCTION	EXAMPLE OF DETAILS TO MATCH
Mike Middleton	Pilot	Hyperprofessional but cannot relate to wife
Joy Middleton	Pilot's wife	Sends texts to husband who won't answer
JT Williams	Copilot	Driven by childhood experiences to be an excellent pilot

↪ *continued on next page*

CHARACTER	FUNCTION	EXAMPLE OF DETAILS TO MATCH
Bobby "Dale" Lee	Navigator	Evacuated from Saigon as a child
Martin "Jeff" Jefferson	Flight Engineer	Experienced professional who trains new loadmasters
Ben Quinten	Loadmaster	Responsible for cargo area of aircraft
Dr. Dan Woody	Medical doctor	Wounded in Vietnam
"Win" Wendy Ames	Nurse	Hyperprofessional medical professional
Taylor Webster	Reporter	Seeking a story with a national byline
George Pike	Wounded Ranger	Looks to help wounded soldiers with the next phase of their lives
Carlos "Charlie" Buenavida	Wounded West Point officer	His brother took the blame for an incident that would have ended his career
Connie Rodman	Wounded mechanic	Cannot have children because of her injuries
Roger Martel	Wounded scout	His children refused to see him in the hospital
John Wordman	Chaplain	Caring counselor who is about to leave his profession
Tom "Lefty" Milton	writer-soldier with a hook	Literature major who joined the Army to find something to write about
Mark "Squeeze" Wilson	Wounded soldier with an artificial arm	Easily embarrassed by women
Anthony "Lucky" Santini	Wounded soldier with a high-tech hand	Friendly, but a wary, street-smart character
J. Nicholas	Santa/American Legion member	HOOTERS owner; invites the pilgrims to his restaurant for lunch

➥ continued on next page

CHARACTER	FUNCTION	EXAMPLE OF DETAILS TO MATCH
Gus Gutierrez	VFW Bus Owner	Drives the pilgrims to lunch
Abigail Milton	writer-soldier's mother	Suggests the story the reporter needs

UNDERGRADUATE LEVEL QUIZ

Question 1 (What happened?) as applied to each chapter provides more than enough information to design a simple three to five-question written quiz that will let the teacher know whether the students are reading and understanding assigned pages. Here is a sample quiz about the Prologue.

1 Where does the Prologue take place?
   On a military aircraft on a military route called SR219 over Arkansas.

2 The crew and aircraft in this chapter are on a mission. What is it?
   They are training to fly in formation at low level and pop up to drop supplies to troops on the ground.

3 Is the mission successful?
   Yes. The bundles from Wolf 41 land on the target cross laid out on the ground.

4 What is an In Flight Emergency (IFE) and what causes one in the Prologue?
   An IFE is an emergency on board the aircraft with equipment or personnel or both. The IFE in the Prologue is caused by both smoke in the aircraft, and an

inexperienced crew member who is struck on the head by a fire extinguisher.

5   How is the end of the Prologue connected to the title of the book?

The young command pilot is very professional during the emergency and lands the aircraft right on the centerline, where it and the crew are safe.

6   BONUS: Why does the pilot declare an IFE?

In a flashback, he remembers a previous event in combat where a crew member described wounded in the back as "not good" when they were in fact in danger of dying. Although the loadmaster on this mission suffers only from superficial bleeding, the memory influences the pilot's decision and he lands as a precaution. This passage establishes the flashback as a technique in this book to explain how events from the past influence current decisions and actions by the characters.

ALTERNATIVE UNDERGRADUATE LEVEL ASSIGNMENTS

»   At least as important as understanding what happens is understanding how the parts of the work fit together. Outlining the novel, and showing chapters, major themes, and any key scenes (reversals, etc.) is a good exercise in this regard. This can be a final assignment after the book has been completed, or a cumulative assignment—an outline that expands as various pages/chapters are completed. (See Question 4 [Author's notes] from Chapter 11 for a short example.) Outlining by chapter can serve the additional purpose of demonstrating to students the importance of outlining their own themes before they begin to write.

» Select a chapter, identify a theme in that chapter, and explain how the author applied one specific literary tool or technique to advance that theme. See Question 2 (How did it happen?) of any chapter for assistance in designing this question.

GRADUATE LEVEL ASSIGNMENTS

» Prepare a short summary of a chapter or group of chapters, and analyze how the interaction of characters sets the **tone** and **mood**.

» Select a theme from a specific chapter or group of chapters, and evaluate which literary technique best advances that message. See Question 3 (What difference does it make?) in each chapter for ideas on how to shape similar questions.

QUESTIONS FOR CLASSROOM DISCUSSION

» **Undergraduate Level:** What is the central theme of Chapter 5 "Fixed," and how does it compare or contrast with the themes of the chapters immediately before and after it?

» **Graduate Level:** Evaluate the lessons that various characters learn in Chapter 5. Which is the most important to advancing the overall narrative? Why?

» **Literary Techniques All Levels:** Sections 2, 3, 4 and 5 of this guide provide various terms and concepts used later in the Question 2 (How did it happen?) analysis of each chapter. A useful exercise follows:

› **Know/Understand:** Given a specific literary technique or concept (flashback, foreshadowing, imagery, repetition, etc.), identify places in the text where it is used.

› **Apply:** Select a technique and explain its use. What does it contribute to the reading experience?

› **Analyze:** Select a passage and explain what technique(s) is/are used and how it/they advance a particular theme, or the overall narrative in a selected chapter.

› **Evaluate:** Select a theme or literary technique, and compare how it is advanced in *CENTERLINE* versus another literary work previously studied. Which is better at accomplishing the author's apparent purpose?

GROUP ACTIVITY

This technique is productive with all levels of student learning.

Review the concept of dramatic structure, and the technique of diagramming that structure (see Figure 1. Freytag's Pyramid in Section 4). Working in small groups, diagram the action from a particular chapter. Alternatively, diagram the actions involving a specific character throughout the length of the book. When does the action climb, plateau, turn, descend, etc.? Compare the answers from different groups. What differences in reader perspective exist? Why?

WRITING PROJECTS

The big difference in writing assignments for different levels of student learning is not just the type of question asked (knowledge, analysis, evaluation, etc.), but also the specificity of focus provided and information required.

» **Undergraduate Level:** As a rule, if teachers expect detailed support from undergraduate students, then they should give students a theme or technique to address and a specific part of the text to examine.

» **Graduate Level:** Teachers may require graduate students to select a theme or technique themselves, and trace its development throughout the entire novel.

RESEARCH PROJECTS: APPLY CRITICAL THINKING

» **Undergraduate Level:** Research specific aspects of the novel. For example, the author seems to suggest that one way to relieve the emotional stress of war is to discuss difficult experiences with friends and family. Is there any actual evidence that this is true?

» **Graduate Level:** Research works (books, movies, etc.) with similar themes. For example, compare how *A Farewell to Arms*, *CENTERLINE*, and the movie *The Best Years of Our Lives*, present the theme of wounded warriors coming home . How are they alike? How are they different? Is one more effective than the others? Why?

ROLE PLAYING

This technique is also appropriate for all levels, but works especially well with undergraduates. Pick a character. How would he or she be played in a movie? What is his or her motivation? What is your support from the book? What actor would you select to portray the character? Why?

CREATIVE PROJECTS

Graduate Level: Create an alternative ending for a character in the book. Would this ending better express existing themes or advance a different theme? How? Using what techniques?

ALTERNATIVE SCHOOLS
OF CRITICISM

As explained in Section 1, this guide is written from the perspective of traditional literary analysis. It assumes that a successful work of art combines a coherent message that moves or informs readers with a careful plan that engages readers. The plan is smoothly executed using traditional tools and techniques. Using this guide to analyze and write about *CENTERLINE* will teach students how to examine, evaluate, and write about any work in a traditional way.

Many other schools of literary criticism also exist. Their perspectives range from Greek criticism based on moral considerations or the structure of the work, to economic perspectives (Marxism or Libertarianism), to more recent cultural or feminist approaches. At least a dozen identifiable schools of literary criticism exist. Find an excellent description of them at Purdue University's site https://owl.english.purdue.edu/owl/owlprint/722/.

One of the major points dividing traditional criticism from other perspectives is the traditional assumption that the author is a reliable source concerning what happened in the work and what it means. Much of modern criticism assigns the author no such privilege, and assumes that he or she may be writing in ignorance of important perspective shaping issues like economic division, psychological analysis, or gender bias.

This guide makes no effort to explain or recommend any of these approaches, beyond simply acknowledging their existence. Study them separately and apply them as desired. But any and all approaches can benefit from understanding what the author was trying to accomplish, how he or she intended to do it, and how well they think they have done. Thus, this guide will provide some value to anyone conducting a literary analysis from any perspective.